THIS
WORKS

THIS
WORKS

How to Use Mindfulness to Calm the Hell Down and Just Be Happy

PADDY BROSNAN

HAY HOUSE

Carlsbad, California • New York City
London • Sydney • New Delhi

Published in the United Kingdom by:
Hay House UK Ltd, Astley House, 33 Notting Hill Gate, London W11 3JQ
Tel: +44 (0)20 3675 2450; Fax: +44 (0)20 3675 2451
www.hayhouse.co.uk

Published in the United States of America by:
Hay House Inc., PO Box 5100, Carlsbad, CA 92018-5100
Tel: (1) 760 431 7695 or (800) 654 5126
Fax: (1) 760 431 6948 or (800) 650 5115
www.hayhouse.com

Published in Australia by:
Hay House Australia Ltd, 18/36 Ralph St, Alexandria NSW 2015
Tel: (61) 2 9669 4299; Fax: (61) 2 9669 4144
www.hayhouse.com.au

Published in India by:
Hay House Publishers India, Muskaan Complex, Plot No.3, B-2,
Vasant Kunj, New Delhi 110 070
Tel: (91) 11 4176 1620; Fax: (91) 11 4176 1630
www.hayhouse.co.in

Text © Paddy Brosnan, 2018

The moral rights of the author have been asserted.

The information given in this book should not be treated as a substitute for professional medical advice; always consult a medical practitioner. Any use of information in this book is at the reader's discretion and risk. Neither the author nor the publisher can be held responsible for any loss, claim or damage arising out of the use, or misuse, of the suggestions made, the failure to take medical advice or for any material on third-party websites.

A catalogue record for this book is available from the British Library.

Tradepaper ISBN: 978-1-78817-121-2
E-book ISBN: 978-1-78817-125-0
Audiobook ISBN: 978-1-78817-300-1

Contents

List of Meditations

Acknowledgements

So many people have put huge effort into getting this book out into the world and making me comprehensible, and I offer great gratitude to them all. My thanks to Amy Kiberd, who showed such belief in the book, Michelle Pilley and the entire team at Hay House for their effort, patience and understanding. The fact that you are able to read this book in a coherent form is in large part down to Susan Feldstein, who gave me some guidance in putting the book together, and Sandy Draper who edited *This Works*. However, any mistakes there may be are entirely mine.

Thanks too is due to Susan and Paul, my agents, who saw some merit in what I had to say and put their reputation on the line by agreeing to represent me.

My family – Faye, Tiernan and Odhrán – are due a lot of thanks too. They have sacrificed many hours in bed, getting up at 4 a.m. to help at my workshops which in many ways form the basis for this book. Without their hard work, patience, support and belief I wouldn't be able to do this work. For this and the many other gifts they have given me, I love them dearly.

The thousands of people who have attended my workshops have taught me so much, and to them I am also very grateful.

I am fortunate to have friends who accept my strangeness and sometimes even encourage it – thank you!

Of course, nothing in this book is particularly original and my greatest debt of gratitude is to my teachers. Some I have had the great privilege of meeting – the Venerable Panchen Ötrul Rinpoche and the Venerable Thich Nhat Hanh. The presence of these teachers in the world is a gift to all of us. Others, including Dzongsar Jamyang Khyentse and Yongey Mingyur Rinpoche, have contributed greatly to my progress along the path with their teachings. May you all stay until suffering ends.

You are not your thoughts and feelings, you are the awareness in which they exist.

Introduction

Making a Venerable Tibetan Lama Giggle

'There is, so I believe, in the essence of everything, something that we cannot call learning. There is, my friend, only a knowledge – that is everywhere, that is Atman,[1] that is in me and you and in every creature, and I am beginning to believe that this knowledge has no worse enemy than the man of knowledge, than learning.'

SIDDHARTHA, HERMAN HESSE

Several years ago, when I was thinking about offering public workshops on mindfulness, I spent some time at Jampa Ling retreat in Cavan in Ireland. I wanted to be clear about my motivation for wanting to teach and that my intentions came from a place of integrity. Having practised mindfulness for a decade by that time, I'd become increasingly aware of the rise in public popularity of the practice. Surely this could only be a good thing?

But I had noticed too that, with mindfulness, we were doing what we in the West always seem to do with the things we bring here from the ancient wisdom traditions – and that is, making it all so ridiculously complicated. All at once mindfulness had become the buzzword of the moment. Now you could get degrees in mindfulness; you could take and teach courses in MBSR (mindfulness-based stress reduction) or mindfulness-based CBT (cognitive behaviour therapy), or even MIBS (mindfulness for irritable bowel syndrome); universities were setting up Mindfulness departments, as were hospitals in their Psychiatry outpatient units. To be able to talk about mindfulness with any authority, it seemed you now had to be a high-ranking academic or a world-renowned expert: a professor of psychiatry, a clinical psychologist or a distinguished neuroscientist.

Yet one of the things that has always attracted me to the practice is its sheer simplicity. The way mindfulness can help us tap into truths we know at an instinctive level (but often lose sight of), and the fact that it is accessible to everybody. Did I – a radio presenter turned investment advisor turned dog groomer – really have anything to contribute? Could I add something to the debate and, most importantly, could I bring something useful to other people?

On my final day in Cavan, I shared some of my concerns with the Venerable Panchen Ötrul Rinpoche, the distinguished Tibetan Buddhist lama and Spiritual Director of Jampa Ling.

His response to my questions was totally unexpected – and completely enlightening. As soon as I mentioned that universities were now offering Masters degrees in mindfulness and that a lady I'd been talking to about offering courses had asked me for my professional qualifications, Rinpoche collapsed into a fit of giggles, which continued for quite some time. After a while, as I sat in front of him nonplussed, two of his attendants came in to see what was happening. Since he was close to 80 years old at the time, those around him were always vigilant for his welfare. I was glad to see them, as I was beginning to worry that my questions and his response might perhaps have done him some kind of physical harm!

Once Rinpoche caught his breath, he finally managed to say, 'But how on earth would they examine you?' Then he dissolved into another fit of laughter. It was clearly one of the funniest – and most bizarre – things he had heard in a long time.

Rinpoche is an erudite and highly educated man with a number of degrees to his name, including the highest degree in Tibetan Buddhist philosophy (*Geshe Lharampa*), which he was awarded in 1980. While he was living in India, he was entrusted by the Dalai Lama with the task of redesigning the educational programmes for the three largest monasteries there – Drepung, Sera and Ganden. There was nothing in Rinpoche's laughter that expressed derision for education or human learning. But what he understood instinctively was that mindfulness is not something that can be related to at a purely intellectual, let alone an academic, level. It is an interior and highly personal process which can only be mastered through an individual practice; it is something simple but very profound which touches the essence of each person's experience of reality. And above all, mindfulness is a way of being whose practice and benefits are accessible to everyone, including me – a radio presenter turned investment advisor turned dog groomer; including you and anyone else reading this book.

I have the greatest of respect for Oxford University and its Department of Psychiatry, for the University of Massachusetts Medical School and the University of California; and for the wonderful work undertaken by these institutions in recent years. However, it is my personal conviction that, for the vast majority of us, bringing interpersonal neurobiology into the picture when we are trying to get to grips with mindfulness is about as useful as studying a set of chemical principles and interactions in order to get a handle on the experience of falling in love.

You don't need degree-level understanding of human biochemistry to know that you're in love; you don't need to read an academic treatise on humour to know that you find something funny. And you certainly don't need to be a neuroscientist or have a deep understanding of the workings of the human brain to experience the profound benefits that practising mindfulness and developing awareness will bring to your life.

Rinpoche's laughter that day was in many ways the biggest affirmation he could have given me just then, and it's something I think back to at times when doubt sets in and I question the extent of my usefulness to my workshop attendees. While it is heartening to see that science is now catching up and adding its weight to some ancient truths, it is also encouraging to know that you don't have to be any kind of scientific expert to be able to enjoy the positive benefits of living your life with awareness.

I hope that this book will be as useful as possible to as many people as possible. I hope that you too will be able to enjoy the huge value that living mindfully can add to your life and come to see that sometimes the simplest things – and actually, the easiest – can also be the most precious.

———

Part I

WHY THIS WORKS

Chapter 1

The Good Stuff

*'Many people are alive, but don't touch
the miracle of being alive.'*
Thich Nhat Hanh

When was the last time you felt frustrated, angry, wound up, stressed out, disappointed, discouraged, depressed, fed up or world weary? Annoyed and irritated with the people around you and really unable to understand why they don't just do what you want them to do – and why they don't automatically know what that is, without you having to tell them all the time?

If you're honest, it probably wasn't that long ago. Some self-help books euphemistically call these feelings 'difficult emotions'; they are what I would call 'personal suffering'. I used to feel all of these things too, frequently and on a regular basis. However, since having a mindfulness practice, I rarely experience emotions of this kind. And when occasionally I do, they are much less intense and distressing than before.

There is nothing special about me, I can assure you. My family will happily attest to this fact. Before I started living mindfully, I was every bit as prone to 'difficult emotions' as anyone else. Some people might even have had me down, on a relative scale, as someone who wasn't particularly easy to live with. I will quite cheerfully put it more bluntly, and say that I was frequently a bit of an ass.

I'll give you an example. If you were to walk into a room at home and see a pair of socks lying on the floor, what would be your first thought? Depending on the kind of person you are and your frame of mind at the time, you might have a range of possible reactions to those socks. Maybe you wouldn't notice them at all – such details are unimportant and don't even register in your field of vision. Maybe your first priority is hygiene, and immediately wonder whether those socks are dirty and need to be washed. Perhaps you're someone to whom order and tidiness are very important, and your first instinct is to pick them up straight away. Or then again, maybe they are the very socks you've been trying to track down for days – and you're just pleased that you've finally found them.

A dozen or so years ago, if I had walked into a room and seen a pair of socks lying on the floor, I would have felt really angry. Although I would never have physically acted out on my anger, I would have made certain that those living in the house with me were left in no doubt about the fact that I was not happy and the degree of my displeasure. The way I saw things at the time, a pair of discarded socks – recently worn and not even paired together before being thrown onto the floor – was a sure and certain sign that those sharing my space had zero respect for me and no regard whatsoever for my feelings. I would have seen it as an affront to my dignity as a person; as proof that the person who'd left the offending objects lying on the floor hadn't given me a second thought.

A pretty extreme reaction, I'm sure you'll agree. Other things, which again to someone else might seem trivial and hardly worthy of notice, would have provoked similarly strong feelings in me... Opening the kitchen cupboard, for example, to find that the clean cups had been put back in a careless, higgledy-piggledy fashion, and not the precise, ordered way I like to stack them myself. Going into the downstairs bathroom and seeing a pair – or even a couple of pairs – of shoes beneath the sink, just left lying wherever they'd been taken off, rather than being put away in their proper place (in the shoe rack in the hall, beside the front door). And so on...

But I guess we all have our pet hates and personal foibles – and maybe mine, and my reactions to them, weren't as odd or over the top as I might imagine, compared to some other people's. Yet even at the time, I was aware that reacting so strongly and, in many ways irrationally, to such relatively minor things, I was creating suffering for those around me, as well as for myself. I certainly knew I wasn't happy, living in such a reactive way.

So, what changed? Well, unlike some people, I didn't have a big, earth-shattering 'Road-to-Damascus' moment that I can still pinpoint in my memory, all these years later. I didn't hit some kind of rock bottom or have a dark night of the soul; there was no time of great personal crisis which forced me all of a sudden to make sweeping changes in my way of being. I am certainly not discounting the value of such transformative experiences, which I know have produced some of the most important insights and realizations for some of those that we have come to regard as luminaries in the field of spirituality and personal growth. (Eckhart Tolle and his park bench in Russell Square come to mind here, for example.) In fact, perhaps my personal story would make better, far more dramatic, reading if I were able to recount something along those lines!

For me, I guess it was more of a slow, progressive realization over time that I wanted things to change and I'd come to the point where I was actively looking for the means to make this happen. Significantly too, it was also around this time that my wife, Faye, and I found out that we were expecting our first child (our son, Tiernan). This news reinforced my resolve that I didn't want to be 'that' person any more – the one who could be so quickly thrown off balance by the sight of a stray pair of socks lying on the living room floor, or a couple of untidily stacked cups in the kitchen cupboard. I knew having a child in the house would mean a whole lot more chaos, but I didn't want to be the kind of assh*le father – or partner – who would kick up a stink about matters of such little importance in the grand scheme of things.

This is when I first began looking into the practice of mindfulness, and I found that it struck an immediate chord with me. I was amazed that something so simple could have such a powerful effect on my life, and relatively quickly too. While I still have the occasional lapse, I can honestly say that for some years now, I have no longer been 'that' person.

'Well, your dad...'

A small incident recently, involving my son Tiernan – who is now 10 years old – brought home to me the extent of my progress since I first started my practice. It was a Saturday afternoon a few months ago, and I was travelling with Tiernan and some of his friends on the team bus back from a rugby match they had just played. Tiernan – who, like his father, is a huge rugby fan – is on the local junior town team, and along with some of the other dads, I like to accompany the boys on their away games whenever I can, to provide some encouragement and moral support.

On this occasion, I was sitting behind Tiernan and one of his close pals, Rory, and couldn't help overhearing some snippets of their conversation on the journey home. At one point, during a typical one-upmanship type of exchange between 10-year-old boys, they began to compare dads.

'Well, your dad's bald,' Tiernan's friend was saying.

'That's 'cos my dad's a Buddhist – so he has to be bald,' came Tiernan's reply. I guess I was touched that he was defending me, although I couldn't entirely condone the little white lie. (I'm not bald because I am a Buddhist; I'm bald because I've lost my hair.)

'OK, but my dad has got loads of hair – even if most of it is grey now,' Rory said.

'Well, that's true,' said Tiernan. 'But at least my dad is really calm, and doesn't keep kicking off all the time, like yours does!'

I didn't actually hear what Rory's comeback to that one was. I was too busy feeling delighted about what my son had just said – which to me was the best kind of confirmation that my years of hard work, practising mindfulness and developing awareness, have definitely had a very positive knock-on effect for those close to me.

> *'The ultimate value of life depends upon awareness and the power of contemplation rather than upon mere survival.'*
> Aristotle

A special practice

While there is nothing special about me, there is something very special about the practice of mindfulness and the subtle changes in perception that it can bring about and transform the way we live. I have tried to give you a sense of the ways in which practising mindfulness has enabled me to live less reactively in everyday situations, and to suffer less as a result. However, this is only a very small part of the picture when it comes to the benefits of developing awareness.

As I mentioned in the Introduction, there is nothing complicated about mindfulness. In fact, you will find these pages contain everything you need to be able to practise mindfulness, live mindfully and free yourself from a lot of suffering. There are just two basic elements to mindfulness – formal meditation and the work of bringing mindfulness into your everyday life. We will look at these in depth in the early chapters of this book.

However, unlike the approaches advocated by so many leading practitioners in recent years, my focus in the greater part of this book won't be on the ways you can use mindfulness to cope with one specific problem or manage one particular issue – anxiety, depression, insomnia, stress, IBS and so on. To my thinking, that would be like giving you a bandage every time you cut yourself, instead of helping you address and deal with *why* you're cutting yourself in the first place. Mindfulness is so much more than just a system or a set of techniques – it is a way of living. It is not something you do – it is something that you are. We practise mindfulness in order to live with awareness, and in living with awareness, we get to experience life fully, directly, for the miracle that it is.

Practising mindfulness in order to live with awareness is of far greater, more holistic value than merely mastering a series of skills to help you handle one particular difficulty. Simply passing on such techniques, without making you aware of the wonderful, life-enhancing effects and benefits that living mindfully can bring, would be like giving you a brand-new car, parking it in your drive and suggesting that you sit in it whenever things get too noisy or stressful in your house! You might get some temporary relief from using your new car as a place of refuge – somewhere to escape to when the going gets tough – but as soon as you step out of it and go back inside again, you'll find yourself back to square one, in the same old stressful situations and enduring the same familiar suffering.

What a pity, if you were to never know that there is so much more you could do if you learned to drive that car – so many new places you could go and fresh things you could experience. Living in awareness through the practice of mindfulness is the equivalent of being able to drive that new car, and being truly free at last to explore the myriad of rich experiences and wealth of possibilities this world and this life has to offer.

Practising mindfulness has enabled me to suffer less in everyday situations; however, as I have indicated, there is so much more to it than that. I can honestly say that developing awareness to the extent that it has become my natural way of being, has transformed my life at every level. My close relationships are richer and more profound; my interactions with everyone I encounter are so much more honest, more real and more enjoyable than before. I now experience deep emotions – like love and grief and joy – more directly and more purely, in a way which is no longer limited by my own narrow preoccupations of self-interest and ego. I am able to move through life with a new sense of freedom, to enjoy people and experiences as I find them and as they actually are, rather than seeing everything 'through a glass, darkly', to use the words of the Bible verse (*1 Corinthians 13:12*) – that is, through the complex filter of my own learned fears and past prejudices. Most wonderful of all, perhaps, I experience deep joy in small, everyday, ordinary things because I carry with me a sense of the miracle of simply being alive and being here, in this moment.

In this book, then, I would like to look at some of the most important aspects of the transformation which awareness makes possible for all of us – and show you just what your brand-new car is capable of.

Before we begin...

There are two final things to say before we begin. First, while I mentioned earlier that I am a Buddhist, there is no sense in which you have to become a Buddhist too, in order to learn how to live mindfully and develop awareness. I am not asking you to give up any of the beliefs you hold or to replace them with something else. While I will refer to some of the wonderful teachers I am lucky enough to have as mentors, and share some of the most relevant lessons and insights they have passed on to me, I will not go any further into the core philosophy of Buddhism or expect you to take any of its tenets on board. Living mindfully is for all of us – regardless of who we are, where we live and what we believe. Thich Nhat Hanh, one of my teachers, said this so much better than I can in *The Miracle of Mindfulness*:

> *'One's breath, after all, is hardly attached to any particular creed.'*

The other very important point is that, if you are new to mindfulness, there may be times when you may not immediately get a sense of the full meaning of what I am saying. Not due to any shortcoming on your part, but because it is only by experiencing some of these things for yourself that you will truly understand them. When this happens, simply try to go with me in these moments and trust that you will, in the course of time and with your own practice, come to deeply know these things for yourself, in the same way you know that you are hungry or that you are in love.

All that remains now is for you to step into this brand-new car, fasten your seatbelt and get ready to enjoy the journey!

———

Chapter 2

Types of Awareness and a New Way of Seeing Things

'[The Buddha is saying that] you only have to know what you are, how you exist; that's all. Just understand your mind: how it works, how attachment and desire arise, how ignorance arises, where emotions come from. It is sufficient to know the nature of all that; just that gives so much happiness and peace. Your life changes completely; everything gets turned upside down; what you interpreted as horrible becomes beautiful.'

LAMA YESHE

Very few of us would argue with the observation that young children experience the world differently to us adults. Anyone who has spent time in the company of a four-year-old will know that they live with spontaneity, a lack of reserve and a sense of 100 per cent immersion in the present, which you will rarely find in an adult. Within the innocent perspective of a small child, every new experience seems completely fresh and exciting; yesterday's tears and tomorrow's trials are quickly, completely and gloriously forgotten in a total engagement in the present moment. When is the last time you heard a five-year-old say, 'I'm very concerned about the events of last Tuesday', or a six-year-old confide, 'You know, I'm really worried about my performance as an octopus in the school play next Wednesday'?

For a child, feelings of happiness and sadness, joy and anger come and go – lived very intensely in the moment, they are fully accepted and unquestioned, neither are they held on to, as they quickly give way to the next experience. There is no worry; there are no feelings of guilt or self-reproach; there are no punishingly high, self-imposed standards to be met next time around. We adults could learn a lot from these wonderful little beings!

Time and again, children bring us back to the joy to be had from fully engaging in what is happening right now. As the father of two young boys, I constantly find myself on the receiving end of this teaching.

Leaving the passenger door open

I remember clearly, for example, one time when Odhrán, our younger son, was about four years old, and I'd just given him the surprise gift of a toy truck that he'd admired a few days earlier in the local toy store. He was over the moon of course, tore open the box and wanted to start playing with his truck straight away. He wanted me to join in and beckoned me to get down on the floor beside him.

'Daddy, you've to get into my new truck with me, and then we're going to drive into Dublin, very fast, on the motorway.'

'That's great, Odhrán – yes, I'll come with you. Let's go!' I said, as I knelt down on the floor too. 'Vroom, vroom,' I chimed in with him, mimicking the sounds of the truck engine, as we tore down the road.

After a few moments of this, I looked at Odhrán, grinning. 'Hey, isn't this cool, son? We're on our way to Dublin in your brand-new truck. What are we going to do when we get there, do you think?' I'm really getting into the spirit of it all now, *I found myself thinking.* What a great father I am!

'We're going to get wood, of course. But you've left your door open, Daddy – you have to close it! Quickly!'

That brought me right out of my self-congratulation. Looking at the passenger door of the truck, I saw that it was in fact closed. But this wasn't the point for Odhrán, of course. The point was that my son was so immersed in the moment, and our drive to Dublin in his new truck, that it was all completely real to him – as it should have been to me too, if I'd really been getting fully into the spirit of it all.

People I've recounted this incident to have remarked that my son must have a very vivid imagination (as indeed a lot of young children do). But I tend to see it rather as a measure of his – or any small child's – ability to be 100 per cent engaged in what they are doing at any given moment, rather than a *mere observer* of it and therefore not mindfully engaged with the present moment.

As such encounters show, young children live mindfully as their natural way of being – i.e. with moment-by-moment awareness of their thoughts, feelings, bodily sensations and outside environment. In this sense, they have a lot to teach us. Perhaps this is what Jesus meant when he said to his followers: 'Truly I tell you, unless you change and become like little children, you will never enter the kingdom of heaven.' [*Matthew 18:3*]

The joy of experiencing directly

One of the many gifts developing and living with awareness brings us is the ability to experience the world and what happens in it through the eyes of a child – in the most positive sense. We see everything anew – fresh, as if for the first time. We find wonder in the things we as adults so often take for granted – the clouds in the sky, the leaves on the trees, the sun, the moon, the breaking of day and the falling of night. We see people as they actually are – ever-changing, multi-faceted beings – rather than through a mesh of our own preconceptions, fears, prejudices, petty resentments and hang-ups. Each day is a new start, as we break out of the constraints of our self-created routines and attempts to control the world. We are ready to accept life for what it is, as it unfolds. We find that we are more open to being surprised, delighted, entertained – as well as being more accepting of the less positive aspects of our experience too, which is a liberation in itself.

There is huge joy, and immense freedom, in being able to just experience things as they are. Consider for a moment what happens when we perceive anything with our senses – when, for example, we smell a flower, or see a leaf or encounter another person. For a millisecond nothing happens: we just perceive the object or the person exactly as they are.

But then almost straight away, thought grabs hold of the thing. The leaf becomes a leaf we don't like the colour of; the flower is our favourite flower, reminding us of happy times; and the person becomes the person who annoyed us the last time we were in their company. The truth is that we almost never experience just what's actually there, without immediately labelling it, or judging it, or attaching an opinion or past association to it.

> Yet the more we are able to drop all of this, and just experience things directly, the less our suffering will be.

As we build and develop our awareness, through formal mindfulness practice and by bringing an attitude of awareness into our daily lives, we discover more about the true nature of reality and grow in our capacity to appreciate life more fully, more deeply. In the simplest terms, awareness allows us to lift the veil of thought from our experience of reality. Going back to the flower or the leaf or the person, you can see that in the usual way of things, we experience everything through a layer of opinions, prejudices, past experience and expectations. We're not encountering the object – we are experiencing our own view of it, which may be very different from someone else's. This can be problematic of course – how can you reach a consensus about an object, if you see it entirely differently from someone else? How can you be sure that you are ever relating to experience as it really is?

It all becomes really challenging however, when it comes to people and how we perceive them and relate to them. How can you have a joyful relationship with anyone, if all you can see is your own prejudices, expectations and opinions? You can't, of course. That person will inevitably end up disappointing you, since they are not what you have decided they are, or what you want them to be – they just are. This is so often the source of our greatest suffering in relationships with others.

True awareness allows us to see just what's there. It gives us the ability to hold on to the reality of the person or the thing or the situation, and to stop thought from adding its layers. It helps us to reduce unnecessary suffering and to enjoy other people, or things, or circumstances, just as they are; for who or what they are.

Types of thought

When I talk about 'thought' in this context, it's important to be clear what I mean. As we know, human beings are capable of many different kinds of thought – analytical, imaginative, creative, contemplative and so on. Psychologists and neuroscientists all recognize this, and many have made considerable efforts to identify and catalogue each of these different types of thinking. But no consensus has yet been reached about exactly how many categories there are, and what these consist of. Some psychologists have, for instance, identified as many as 39 distinct modes of thinking – but, as I have said, this number is not necessarily definitive.

Many of our modes of thinking are of course potentially constructive – particularly creative thought (if used for a good end), analytical thought (which helps us learn from our experiences) and contemplative thought (helping us to integrate our experiences in a useful, constructive way). Often when people talk about 'thought' in the context of mindfulness, the subtext is that it is largely a negative, potentially destructive thing, something which leads to suffering. But as I have said, there are lots of types of thought and many of them actually enhance our lives.

In this book, when I talk about thought in the context of awareness and mindfulness, I'm referring specifically to what is known as 'default mode' thought. We will be looking at 'default mode' thinking in more detail in the next chapter, but for now we can say that it is the state of our brain being in neutral, when we are not focused on the outside world or fully engaged in a practical or external task. It's the ruminating, or mind-wandering, mode of thinking – which some people refer to as the 'mental chatter' in our heads – that is ongoing when we are not fully immersed in the present moment. Research has revealed that default mode thinking has two main features:

1. We are always unconscious of the thoughts we have when in this mode;

2. The majority of these thoughts – 60 to 70 per cent – are negatively biased.[2]

Studies have established that we spend about 55 per cent of our waking hours in default mode.[3] Which means that for over half our lives, we have no control over our thinking; and that this thinking, since it's largely negative, is a destructive force, which can – and does – negatively affect our behaviour, judgement and performance on a daily basis.

So, this is what I mean by 'thought' in the context of mindfulness – the ongoing, generally neurotic inner monologue in our heads of which we are unaware, but which wastes a lot of our mental energy and time, and causes much of our suffering. We will look in the next chapter at how the practice of mindfulness actually works to slowly but surely reduce the length of time we spend in default mode.

Awareness

As with thought, there are many types and levels of awareness – developing our awareness is a never-ending, always unfolding, process. Here, to start off with, I'd like to take you through some of the key stages of awareness, and the ways in which your life will be enhanced as you manage to arrive at them through your mindful practice. The key thing about awareness, as I have said earlier, is that it enables us to lift the veil of thought from reality and experience life as it really is.

It's important to note here that, although I am talking in terms of stages, I am mainly doing so for ease of reference and as a simple way to introduce these ideas to you. The reality is that the development of awareness doesn't necessarily happen in any particular, prescribed sequence – you may gain any of these insights in any order and at any time, separately or indeed all together. There is no sense in which you must attain the first 'stage' before being able to get to the other stages. Indeed rather than stages, the types of awareness I am talking about here are more like a number of different insights – glimpses into the true nature of life and reality.

Stage 1: Obvious awareness

The first level of awareness which living mindfully allows us is the ability to recognize more quickly the physical sensations we experience when going through certain emotions. With further practise, we will then be able to identify, and challenge, the thoughts and core beliefs that lie behind these emotions. I often refer to this when I teach as 'obvious' awareness, by which I mean that it's the most direct, immediate and easily accessed kind. If we can develop this capacity, we are able to identify feelings as they arise, and – in time and with practice – to short-circuit them before they completely take hold of us and compel us to act out in ways that will cause suffering to ourselves and others.

I'll give you an example of what I mean in the following story – one I often use in my workshops. In fact, people who come to see me speak more than once will sometimes ask me to tell it again – perhaps because it's a situation so many of us can relate to. It goes something like this:

The husband and the bread

It's a busy weekday early morning in the O'Brien household, as Mary serves breakfast to the three kids. Her husband Joe, who has to leave the house earlier than anyone else, is taking the last few gulps of his tea, as he checks he's got enough change in his pockets for the toll bridge out of Dublin.

'Have a good day, love,' Mary says, as Joe gives her a peck on the cheek and says goodbye. 'Oh – I nearly forgot – could

you get us a loaf of bread on your way home later? I've to make the kids their lunch for tomorrow, and I'll probably give them a few slices of toast before they head off to football training tonight.'

'No problem, Mary,' Joe replies. 'I'll call into the shop on my way back. Not a worry.'

'Thanks. You won't forget now, will you? You know what the boys are like if they don't get their toast before the game.'

'Not a bother, love, I won't forget – you know that.'

'OK, that's great. Now, you'd better get going or you'll be late!'

All well and good. Mary has a bit of a stressful morning though, one way and another – her day just seems to be one long 'to do' list that never ends. At lunchtime, she's already thinking of all the stuff she'll have to take care of later that evening. Remembering the bread, she decides to send Joe a quick text, which she knows he'll get during his lunch break.

'Hiya hon – hope you're having a good day? Don't forget the bread later. x'

Joe texts straight back – he's good that way. 'No worries – I'm on it. Love u.'

The afternoon goes by quickly, and soon the three boys are back from school already and getting themselves ready for football practice at 5:30 p.m.

'I'm starving, Mam – and there's no bread left! Where's my toast? I always have toast before practice...', the middle one, who's 10, grumbles.

'Never mind, love – your Dad'll be back any minute, and he's bringing fresh bread with him. Won't be long now.'

Just then, Joe comes in the front door. He makes his way straight to the kitchen to see everybody, as usual. He's had a good day – news of a pay rise and he has a day's leave, the day after tomorrow, so he's got a big smile on his face.

'Hiya, love,' Mary greets him. 'How was your day—?' she starts, but then she registers that he's standing there empty-handed. 'Where's the bread? I hope you got my bread, Joe!'

'Ah now, don't tell me. I forgot the bread—'

'What?! Didn't I send you a text at lunchtime, you stupid eejit? What am I supposed to do now? Couldn't you even think of me for one single minute?'

At this point, all hell breaks loose. Mary is beside herself with anger. She has three starving boys to feed within the next half hour. And then there's the lunches later – making the sandwiches for school is usually the last thing on her list for the day – and now that numbskull husband of hers has forgotten to pick up the bread.

Soon Mary has lost it completely and she's in full rant mode. The three boys look on in shocked silence, as she berates poor Joe – even questioning why he bothered to marry her in the first place, if all he was ever going to do was be so selfish and not listen to the simplest thing she says.

After a while, Mary is feeling a little shocked herself at just how angry she is. Why is she getting so worked up over a simple loaf of bread, and the fact that Joe made the easy mistake of forgetting to stop at the shop on his way home? She knows she forgets things too sometimes – everybody does. Why is she making such a big deal about this?

By the time she finally begins to calm down, there are five very upset people in the house. Joe has had about all he can take. All at once, he turns on his heel and just walks out of the kitchen and then the front door, slamming it behind him. In floods of tears, Mary collapses into a chair at the kitchen table, bewildered at how things have escalated into this. The youngest of the boys tries to cling on to her, sniffling dejectedly. The two older boys have given up all notion of going to football and retreat to the room they share, where they switch on the TV and turn up the volume – loud.

Perhaps this seems like an extreme example – but is it really? Most of us have probably had similar kinds of experiences, when our nearest and dearest don't live up to our expectations, or do the seemingly small things we ask. Some kind of minor domestic issue arises and suddenly, out of nowhere – or so it seems – tempers flare and an argument erupts. Both sides end up saying things they'll later regret, often raking up past demeanours of the other person that everyone thought were long forgiven and forgotten. And then you find yourself in the same situation as Mary, wondering how on earth something as trivial as a loaf of bread has become important enough to rock your relationship with one of the people you're supposed to love most in the world.

Of course for Mary, the loaf of bread isn't the real issue at all. Part of her realizes this, since she registers that she's taken aback at the depth of her own anger. But she doesn't have sufficient awareness – of where the anger came from and why she has reacted in such a disproportionate way – to be able to deal with the situation in a more measured, reasonable and constructive way, causing less suffering for everyone involved – including, of course, herself. Wouldn't it have been so much better if she'd managed to short circuit her anger, express her annoyance quickly and then move on, by asking Joe to go out and get the bread as soon as possible?

Recognizing the physical signs of emotions

If Mary had been practising mindfulness and working on developing awareness, she would have been able to sense the feeling of her anger building up much earlier. She would have been more tuned in to her own immediate physical sensations – the burning in the pit of her stomach, the increasing tension in her neck and shoulders and across her chest, her heart thumping. She would have identified these feelings quickly as irritation and impatience, long before they became rage. She could have bought herself some time – between registering the feeling of anger and verbally lashing out at Joe, and so upsetting everyone in the house.

In that mental and emotional space, depending on her level of awareness, Mary might even have been able to pinpoint the thoughts at the root of her rage, and realized that these thoughts had no real basis in reality. For example, the idea that Joe doesn't care about her; the thought that she's not important enough to him; and even, at the bottom of it all, the notion that she's not a good or nice enough person to deserve her husband's – or anyone's – love and respect. The kind of destructive, toxic thoughts which our constant mental chatter, our unconscious default mode, would have us buy into and believe. It's hardly any wonder that Mary felt so angry and hurt, is it?

So, the first level of awareness we can attain through the practice of living mindfully allows us this: the ability to quickly connect with our feelings and emotions in intense situations, and to create enough mental space to be able to work out what's really going on; to distinguish between fact and fantasy. This enables us to act – rather than *react* – in ways which are constructive and cause the least amount of suffering to ourselves and other people. Awareness gives us the power to choose how to respond to what happens to us – rather than just being at the whim of our emotions, feelings and skewed beliefs about ourselves and the world.

As far as emotions go, some teachings propose that there are basically only two key emotions – love and fear – and that all other feelings are ultimately derived from these. Love and fear do indeed represent two very different, opposing impulses, or responses, to life. Many of our negative, destructive feelings – such as anger, envy, resentment, hatred and so on – can be seen as stemming from fear, while love is essentially the desire to connect and gives rise to our most positive feelings – such as joy, empathy, compassion, respect, affection and so on.

Stage 2: Subtle awareness

The practice of mindfulness – which we will look at in depth in the next two chapters – involves cultivating a non-judgemental and neutral 'watchfulness' of our feelings, thoughts and bodily sensations as they come and go. As we continue to practise and bring a mindful quality of attention into our everyday lives, broader and more profound levels of awareness become possible.

One thing we become increasingly conscious of is the extent to which each of us sees life, and experiences everything that happens to us as individuals, through a very complex set of filters. These filters are our own opinions, prejudices, past experiences and expectations, fears and illusions – and even, as we have seen in the example of Mary and Joe, the deep-seated and often unconscious beliefs we hold about ourselves.

The purpose of a photographic filter is to change the image that has been captured by the camera – and the effect of our own metaphorical filters of thought and belief is the same. These alter and distort the way we see and experience life, changing what is there to be directly perceived into something altogether different.

I find it helpful to think of these mental filters as a series of grey photographic filters, placed one on top of the other, which together create a thick screen that, as we look through it, largely obscures whatever object we are viewing. What deeper levels of awareness allow us to do is to identify and then lift away these filters one by one – until ultimately, we are able to perceive reality directly and without any distortion. We see and experience our lives, and especially the people around us, as they really are.

It is only when you become more aware that you realize how strange, and unhelpful, some of your own filters really are. Each of us will have our own unique set of biases and 'notions', of course. A fairly bizarre one of mine used to be that all Asian people must be good at maths. I haven't a clue where this idea came from originally, but I do know that, like most preconceptions, it isn't always borne out in real life! Other more run-of-the-mill prejudices include the notions that an older person who is hard of hearing is somehow less intelligent; that overweight people are likely to be lazy; that women drivers aren't as competent as male drivers – and so on.

The idea I had about Asian people and maths seemed harmless, if a little strange. However, for as long as I was unaware of it, the potential for problems was there. An incident which happened during my time working in financial services illustrates this point well.

Bizarre filters

Finding myself faced with a fairly complex spreadsheet calculation, I decided to call on a colleague from Taiwan for some help. I emailed him the figures, explained my difficulty and asked if he could be of assistance. After about an hour however, he emailed me back, saying that he'd had a look and couldn't figure it out either. I felt really annoyed with him, as I was absolutely convinced that he just didn't want to help me. The names I called him in my head were unkind – to say the least!

Looking back, I realize that my anger was due to the bizarre filter through which I viewed this guy. One that absolutely believed that, because he was Asian, he was good at maths and could easily help me but just couldn't be bothered. This of course was nonsense, but it still led me to think of him negatively and it definitely affected our working relationship. He had never demonstrated a flair for maths and I had no actual reason for believing he had one. I had singled him out to help me with my calculation problem because of my own distorted view, which of course he couldn't possibly live up to.

Awareness allows you to catch your automatic thoughts and assumptions as they arise, and to challenge them by determining whether they have any basis in reality. As you catch and then identify these thoughts, you may also find yourself laughing at their sheer absurdity. You may also find yourself taken aback by what they reveal about your long-held, but unconscious, beliefs about the world and other people.

I remember clearly one occasion some years back now, when I got an unexpected glimpse into another of my own automatic, default mode thoughts. I was in our back garden, hanging out some of the family's washing on the clothes line. Hardly the most dramatic of circumstances, as I'm sure you'll agree – and yet the insights I gained gave me a lot to think about, so I'll share it with you.

Hanging out the washing

Hanging out the washing is one of those household chores I share with my wife. Faye generally leaves for work earlier than me in the mornings, and so if there's any laundry to be hung out, I'll be the one to do it, if I have time. I'd already noticed that it was one of those tasks that I always seemed to rush through, regardless of whether I was in a hurry or not. I also realized that I wasn't particularly fond of this job, although I had no idea why.

On the morning in question, I was in the process of hanging out quite a big load of laundry, when suddenly I became aware of my thoughts. As if for the first time, I realized that I was feeling harried and actually quite uncomfortable; a feeling very similar to embarrassment, really. I was just hanging out socks and T-shirts, though – not lingerie or underwear, or anything like that! – and I remember wondering why I would possibly be feeling embarrassed.

Then I caught this thought: I'll bet your man from next door can see me doing this – standing here, first thing in the morning, with my clothes pegs and the family laundry in a basket at my feet... And I'll bet he's thinking to himself, 'Ah now, look at him – he mustn't be working at the moment, and she's had to give him stuff to do during the day to keep him busy. Sure, isn't he well under the thumb? That's women's work, really, but I guess she reckoned, if he's got nothing else to do, he might as well be the one to do it.'

Suddenly I realized what was really going on. I was projecting my own ideas and feelings onto our poor, unsuspecting neighbour (who, I am sure, could not have cared less what I was doing or why I was doing it). It was highly unlikely that he was looking out of his window at that precise moment and thinking these things about me. (And of course, even if he was, what did it really matter to me?)

It was clearly not my neighbour, but me who was thinking, deep down, that hanging out laundry to dry was a woman's job rather than a man's, and that the fact that I was doing it was some kind of affront to my male dignity and something about which I felt slightly ashamed! It was me, Paddy, who felt that I should have been out working or doing something more 'manly', and that I should have refused to do this menial task.

As someone who has always regarded himself as liberal, open-minded and very much in favour of equality of the sexes, it was a slight shock to discover these ideas at the heart of my thinking. Did I really hold such traditional, chauvinistic views and think that certain household chores were the domain of women? Did I really feel that my role as a man should be to be out in the world doing something more important and worthier of my time, in the more traditional sense? And what did this say about how I saw Faye's place in the world and in the family?

Once I got over the initial shock of this realization, I actually found myself laughing – at the ridiculousness of my thoughts, at my feelings of embarrassment about the idea of being seen by other men to be doing something apparently so unworthy. For sheer silliness, really, it was hard to credit! And yet for years, this is what had been going around in my mind, albeit without my conscious knowledge.

After that, I found that I was no longer in such a mad rush to hang out the washing. I was able to do it in a much looser, more relaxed way now that my mind was free of my previous daft anxieties about what the neighbours might be thinking. Since then, I've been able to just focus on the job at hand, take the air and enjoy a few moments outside in the calm of the garden.

A new freedom

As you tune in more and more to your own distorted ideas about life and other people, and focus more on the unbiased observation of what is really happening – moment to moment – you will find that many of your filters simply fall away of their own accord. You'll discover that there is a tremendous freedom in just being able to enjoy people for who they really are. You no longer risk suffering disappointment since you're no longer holding someone up to an unrealistic version of who you think, or would like to imagine, they are or should be. You no longer reproach them for not living up to an ideal you've imposed on them, and which they had no part in creating. Hence their suffering as well as yours will be dramatically reduced. By accepting people for themselves, you allow for and in a way, actually create the possibility for transformation. Things are no longer rigid or fixed, predictable and static – everything is up for change!

Stage 3 and beyond: Deeper levels of awareness

As you continue to practise mindfulness and bring its special quality of attention into your everyday life, your awareness will continue to expand in all sorts of surprising and wonderful ways. You will discover that your likes and dislikes, or biases and preferences no longer dictate your behaviour. You no longer react habitually, but instead find yourself more and more able to act on the basis of true choice and rationality.

With further mindful practice, you'll grow more accomplished in the art of simple observation. You'll start to simply experience what is in front of you, without rushing to judge, over-analyse or categorize your thoughts and impressions, in the way you would previously have done as a matter of course. Most significantly, you'll begin to notice that your perspective has shifted in an important way. Now you are able to watch your thoughts, rather than being completely consumed by them. Now you are not the thinker, you are just witnessing a stream of thoughts. You no longer identify with your thoughts as being your essential self, all of who you are. And you'll come to realize that, while these thoughts might be generated by some part of you, they do not represent the entirety of your being or the full extent of your consciousness.

This realization will afford you a wonderful sense of spaciousness – between your feelings and thoughts; between your intense emotions and the way you choose to respond to them; between stimulus and any action you take in response to it. The more you practise mindfulness and develop your awareness, the wider the space becomes, and the greater the ease with which you'll be able to go about your life. In this space, you will also find a sense of oneness, stillness and peace, as well as reservoirs of love and compassion you never knew you had. In fact these were always within you, but only by creating mental and emotional space within yourself are they able to reveal themselves. You will enjoy a new sense of freedom – from the limitations of your entrenched ways of seeing the world and from the bondage of default mode thinking.

Ultimately, as your practice continues and your awareness expands accordingly, you will find that the boundaries of your ego slowly but surely begin to melt away completely. As well as this, your everyday experience, which you carry with you at all times, will be filled with a sense of the infinite connectedness between all things – including between you and the world around you.

We are getting into far deeper levels of awareness now – and what may seem like very abstract territory, especially if you are new to mindfulness practice and living mindfully.

However, this is something we will look at in greater depth, and in more concrete ways, in the later chapters of this book.

Tasting a strawberry and describing the colour blue

As I said at the beginning of this book, it is very difficult to adequately describe this new way of perceiving things. To draw on a traditional analogy from Buddhist teaching, trying to convey the essence of this experience is a bit like trying to describe the taste of a strawberry to someone who has never eaten one or, to give another example, to convey a sense of the colour blue to someone who has never seen it.

Words can only go part of the way to expressing these things; to truly understand, you must live them for yourself. While as far as this goes, I can only try to point you in the right direction, so to speak, I can however describe the effect this kind of clarity of perception has, and the difference it brings to our everyday experience. There is no longer the same anxiety or fear, since there are no expectations. There is no hate or annoyance, since there is no longer any prejudice or bias. There is no longer any challenge to our egos – since we no longer have opinions or pre-existing ideas to be challenged or proven correct.

In short, there is a lot less suffering, and so much more joy!

'I would like to give you one small piece of advice to keep in your heart. All that we are looking for in life – all the happiness, contentment, and peace of mind – is right here in the present moment. Our very own awareness is itself fundamentally pure and good. The only problem is that we get so caught up in the ups and downs of life that we don't take the time to pause and notice what we already have.'

YONGEY MINGYUR RINPOCHE[4]

Part II

PRACTICAL AWARENESS

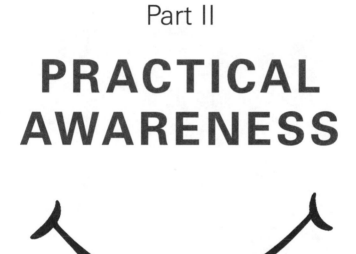

Chapter 3

Journey to Awareness:
20 Minutes Morning
and Evening

*'Meditation practice isn't about trying to throw
ourselves away and become something better.
It's about befriending who we already are.'*

PEMA CHÖDRÖN

One of the first steps on your journey to greater awareness, with all the wonderful benefits this will bring, is to learn how to practise mindfulness. Practising mindfulness, in order to live mindfully, is the key to the shift in perspective that is the starting point for greater awareness, and a new way of seeing things which will transform your life.

A lot has been written and published about mindfulness in recent years – so much so that in many Western countries, the term has now become part of the everyday vocabulary of people from all walks of life. Training in mindfulness is now part of the national curriculum for pupils in primary schools in Ireland; in the UK, mindfulness programmes are becoming increasingly popular across the board; in the public sector, including those working in local government and in education; at a community level, in the form of doctor referrals for mindfulness training; and in private sector businesses.[5] An acquaintance of mine who has recently set up a small private security company that specializes in delivering training for door staff and private security personnel, told me that basic mindfulness training is now a module that many course participants expect to be offered on their course curriculum – and something that today's bouncers and bodyguards are apparently finding invaluable!

It is of course thanks to the pioneering work of Jon Kabat-Zinn, Professor Mark Williams and Jack Kornfield (to name a few) and their science-based approach, that mindfulness as a concept has become so widely accepted and embraced by modern Western society. We live in an age in which our main religions have lost much of their sway and, some would say, credibility, and where there is a general suspicion of other, alternative systems of spirituality. In this context, the science supporting the value of mindfulness, as a way of safeguarding and improving our mental and emotional wellbeing, has won over public opinion with its reassuring clout of rationally based, tangible evidence.

It is therefore likely that many of you will already be familiar with the term 'mindfulness', and have a good sense of what it means. But just to recap:

Mindfulness is the moment-to-moment awareness of your thoughts, feelings and outside environment.

As I stressed in the Introduction, my emphasis in this book is to explore a holistic understanding of mindfulness, i.e. not merely as a set of techniques or a system to address specific problems or issues. In this sense, I will be looking at mindfulness not as something that you *do* – but rather something that you *are*. Mindfulness is a way of living and being, and not just an independent, standalone resource to be drawn upon now and again, whenever particular circumstances or conditions require it. We practise mindfulness in order to live mindfully – that is, in order to live with awareness.

This is a key point which I will keep coming back to throughout the following chapters. In fact, by the time you've finished reading, you may even be fed up with my insistence in saying it! If, however, my constant reiteration means that you take this idea on board fully, then I will happily endure your impatience now and again – since my chief purpose is to be as useful to you as I possibly can be.

Mindful meditation practice is basically a way of gently retraining the mind, and as such is an ongoing learning process. So you might logically ask, why does the mind need retraining? We will explore this concept in more depth in later chapters, but for now the most straightforward answer is that the greater part of the personal suffering we experience on an everyday basis is due to not reacting to things as they really are, but to how we *think* they are, or should be. And how we interpret and feel about what happens to us is greatly determined by the thoughts that we have. So it follows that if we want to enjoy – and not just endure – our lives, we need to rid ourselves of our distorted ways of thinking. And, in turn, of relating to and interacting with the world and the people around us.

To hit you with just a little bit of science, it's been established that the average person has about 60,000 thoughts per day. The greater proportion of these thoughts are not new. In fact studies have established that about 95 per cent of our thoughts are exactly the same as yesterday, and the day before that, and so on. So, we don't generate 60,000 new thoughts per day – but rather recycled versions of old ones, which in turn are based on our existing impressions, prejudices and opinions.[6] This is the way most of us go through life from one day to the next – on autopilot; reprocessing old thoughts, relating and reacting to things based on the way that we've done so in the past, and pretty much condemned to continuing the same old patterns of relating and reacting to things in the future.

As we saw in the last chapter, research reveals that we spend over half of our waking hours in default mode, and that the greater majority of our daily autopilot thoughts are negative; this is our default bias. While, as we have also seen, we are always unaware of the thoughts we're generating in default mode, most of us have an instinctive sense of the predominantly negative nature of these thoughts.

To illustrate my point, I'll give you a common example of this; and one that tends to raise a laugh of recognition from the audience when I mention it in my workshops. When passing a full-length mirror, how many of us are likely to stop and stare at our reflection with admiration and awe, and find ourselves thinking thoughts such as: *My, but I'm looking stunning today! God, but I look SO good – how lucky is the world to have me? People should really just be thanking me for simply being here, looking THIS good!* Perhaps there's the odd person out there with NPD (Narcissistic Personality Disorder), who really does routinely think in this way – but I'd say they are few and far between. For most of us, catching sight of ourselves unexpectedly in a passing mirror will cause our inner critic to go into overdrive: *Look at that double chin I'm getting now... My hair is sitting really badly – talk about a bad hair day! Please don't tell me that's another spot on my chin – why didn't I see it this morning? That shop assistant told me my bum didn't look big in these jeans – well, that was a lie.* And so on and so forth.

It's been established that human beings start to become cognitively and rationally aware at around the age of eight. So, if you are say, 32 years old now, this means that you'll have been forming and consolidating your default mode thought patterns for at least 24 years – which is a long time, when you think about it. When you consider that the majority of the thoughts you've been having are not new and predominantly negative, you'll probably agree when I say that this is potentially an unhelpful, boring and, most importantly, very limiting way to live.

It was Albert Einstein who said, 'There are only two ways to live your life. One is as though nothing is a miracle. The other is as though everything is a miracle.' Retraining your mind gently through mindful meditation practice, in order to live with awareness, means choosing the second option, and opening up your mind to a far more enriching, exciting and rewarding way of living.

Given that, as I've said above, by the time we reach adulthood our ways of thinking are already pretty much entrenched and will become increasingly so as we age, it's not surprising that retraining the mind may take a little time. When learning how to play the guitar, you don't pick up the instrument and find yourself able to strum a series of complex chords immediately – and you wouldn't expect to either. Similarly mindfulness and living with awareness requires some time and effort – and, like any other new skill, practice. This brings me to a second key point:

There's no such thing as the immediate acquisition of mindfulness.

When it comes to gently retraining the mind, in order to change engrained ways of thinking and perceiving, there's some work to be done, especially at first. And yet, when you consider the extent and depth of the changes that will begin taking place within a relatively short space of time, the effort involved is hardly monumental.

As I said in Chapter 1, there are just two basic elements to the practice of mindfulness: formal meditation and the work of bringing mindfulness into everyday life. We will look at the first of these – the formal practice of mindful meditation – now and in the next chapter. In Chapter 5, we'll explore the second element.

Formal meditation

Mindful meditation is the process of becoming aware of the body and mind, so that we can learn about our thought processes and the feelings accompanying them. Through formal meditation, we learn the skills that will enable us to make conscious decisions and choices about how we react to events, our environment and the people around us, instead of being pushed and pulled around by our negative thoughts (most of which we are not even aware of) and the often unhelpful feelings they generate.

Every time you sit in mindful meditation, you'll learn more about yourself and your inner landscape – and then you'll be able to bring what you learn into your everyday life. Eventually, and with practice and repetition, the new ways of thinking and perceiving which you acquire through meditation will become second nature. A scientist would say that this is the process of forging and consolidating new neural pathways in your brain.

I would say that this is the process of becoming aware and experiencing life directly as it is.

If you go to the gym regularly, you'll know that the benefits of physical training don't stop when you finish your session and walk out of the door. In the same way, when it comes to formal mindful meditation, the positive effects don't cease when you get up from your cushion or chair. Instead, they carry over into your everyday life and continue to help you, as you negotiate the things you experience there and the people you interact with.

A crucial point to note here is that mindful meditation is not relaxation, or something that is intended to induce sleepiness (or even unconsciousness in the form of sleep), or to help you 'tune out'. On the contrary, mindful meditation is actually aimed at reaching a state of **focused awareness** – a heightened form of consciousness where you are more intensely in touch with your bodily sensations, your thoughts and your feelings.

20 minutes morning and night

For daily formal meditation practice, you will need to set aside 20 minutes in the morning and 20 minutes in the evening. I recommend that you build up your practice gradually, session by session until you are able to spend the full 20 minutes in meditation. So begin with five minutes, and then start increasing the length of time from there. While 20 minutes might not sound like a lot, if you've never done any kind of formal meditation before, you may find it challenging to try to focus for this length of time when starting off.

Of course, you might very well be thinking that 20 minutes' practice morning and evening is an impossible ask, given how hectic your days at work and home tend to be. How on earth will you possibly be able to find that kind of time to set aside on a daily basis, given all you have to do? If this is your first reaction, I have a couple of questions for you. Are you really saying that your constant presence in your household is so absolutely necessary to those living with you, that everything will grind to a halt and descend into chaos if you go into another room for 20 minutes? And do you really think that making these small adjustments to your day aren't worth the effort, when it comes to transforming how you experience life, and making the most of the short time you're lucky enough to have on this Earth?

> If you want things to be different,
> you have to change something.

When to meditate

A lot of people will claim that their mornings are so hectic, there isn't a chance they'll be able to set aside 20 minutes of calm. If this is the case for you, I have a simple solution to propose: set your alarm the night before so that you wake up 20 minutes earlier than usual the next morning. It's as easy as that!

Some people will also say that they're routinely so tired by the time evening comes around, all they want to do is fall asleep. And that if they take 20 minutes at night to sit calmly in a quiet room, there's every likelihood they'll just fall asleep. This is why I always advise that the best time to meditate at night is certainly *not* just before bedtime – because by then, most of us will indeed be liable to simply fall asleep. Evening meditation should ideally be done when the mind is still alert and not overly tired – so, for most of us, this will be some time between 8 and 9 p.m. I know, you're thinking now that this is when most of the good stuff is on TV – but fortunately, these days, the record or catch-up function on your TV means that you no longer have the dilemma of choosing between meditating and watching your favourite show.

Where to meditate

The best place to meditate is simply somewhere in your home where you can be sure that no one else will interrupt you. So, a quiet room where there's no regular through traffic would be ideal – your bedroom or spare room for example. You certainly don't want to install yourself on the floor in the middle of the living room where the rest of the family are watching TV, and pronounce grandly that you're about to meditate and that no one should under any circumstances speak, move or otherwise interrupt you – as, realistically, that isn't going to happen.

The best position for meditation is to sit with your spine upright (preferably with no support behind your back), your legs crossed and your hands in your lap, and with your left hand cradling your right and your thumbs lightly touching. You want to sit up straight, yet in a relaxed fashion. Never meditate lying down, as again, the most likely thing that will happen is that you'll fall asleep.

Remember, mindful meditation is about reaching a state of focused awareness, not reaching a state of unconsciousness!

In terms of what to sit on, you can use a cushion, a chair or even a stool, just as long as you ensure that you keep your upright posture through your own relaxed attention, rather than by relying on the support of a chair back or the wall. I use two meditation cushions from Tibet – a small *zafu* (round cushion) set on top of a *zabuton* (a larger, square cushion) – as I find this combination is both comfortable and helpful in keeping my posture upright. However, you don't have to get your cushions from Tibet, and it's not obligatory to invest in a *zafu* or *zabuton*, or both. A simple small round cushion will be perfectly adequate for the purpose, as long as it provides enough padding and support to enable you to sit comfortably for 20 minutes or longer.

Finally, remember to put your phone on silent and explain to others in the house that you're not to be interrupted for the next 30 minutes or so. Especially when you start off, it's a good idea to set some kind of gentle alarm or timer to alert you when the 20 minutes (or whatever length of time you choose to start with) is up. (There are lots of meditation timer apps available – just remember to put your phone on silent or 'do not disturb'. The apps will still work regardless.) Otherwise, especially at the outset, you'll probably find yourself looking at the time every few minutes, imagining that the 20 minutes have already passed. As you get more accustomed to spending time in meditation, you will likely reach a point where the time seems to go by in an instant, or indeed you may even lose any sense of time passing at all.

In a monastery, a bell with a deep tone is used for communal meditation sessions. This is usually a 'bowl bell', which is like a singing bowl. Normally the bell is 'invited' to sound twice at the beginning of the session. Traditionally, the first sounding will be a dull, non-resonating thud, which signals to those about to meditate that they should ready themselves; this is followed by a second, much fuller and more resonant reverberation, which marks the beginning of the meditation. At the end of the session, the bell is then rung, or 'invited to sound', once to bring those present out of meditative mode and back to the room.

A final small tip when setting your timer or alarm – make sure the alert tone you choose is a pleasant, gentle one, and it's probably better to avoid the same one you use for your morning alarm, which may have all sorts of other associations for you!

Once you've got these practicalities sorted, you're ready to start meditating. The way that you approach formal meditation practice is very important, and various analogies have been traditionally used to help explain why. When I was being taught the basics of formal practice while on retreat at Jampa Ling, the analogy my teacher gave me, and which I found really helpful, was that of a tightrope. In terms of the best physical stance and mental attitude to adopt while meditating, you are seeking the right balance in several senses: between maintaining your posture, and being physically relaxed at the same time; and between staying sufficiently mentally focused, and not being overly tense or intense. Where balancing on a tightrope is the act of meditating, it follows that if you are too rigid or tense – either physically or mentally – your tightrope will become overly taut, and you will fall off. Conversely, if you are too relaxed and unfocused, the tightrope will become too loose, you may end up falling asleep and, inevitably, fall off.

The tightrope analogy also comes into play regarding your mental attitude to meditating. If during your 'sitting', you come across a thought or feeling or sensation that you don't like, and you accordingly push against it or try to resist it, you will fall off your meditative tightrope. Similarly, if you have a thought or impression that you are enjoying, and you make a conscious effort to try to hold on to it or grasp after it, you will also fall off.

The tightrope image is a really good one for helping us get a handle on this state of balance, or equanimity, that you're trying to maintain while meditating – one where you treat pleasant and unpleasant thoughts in the same way as neutral, unremarkable ones, allowing them all to stay around for as long as they 'want' to, and then go again, and not trying to hurry them away or grab onto them in an attempt to prolong them. You may not believe it, but it won't take you long to reach this balanced meditative state.

Getting started

I generally suggest starting with one of the most important – and simplest – meditations: **Meditation on the Breath**. This is one of the most widely used among Buddhist and non-Buddhist meditators alike, largely for the basic reason that the breath is always available to us – no matter where we are or what situation we find ourselves in.

Before beginning, simply close your eyes, take a deep breath and release it slowly – in and out through your nose. In mindful meditation, we always breathe in and out through the nose. And again, in through the nose and out through the nose. One last time – and this time, as you slowly release the breath, just relax your body. Make sure your shoulders are not hunched up, but relaxed; check that you are not clenching your fists or your jaw; ensure your eyes are lightly closed, rather than being screwed tightly shut.

Meditation on the Breath

Begin with sound. With your eyes closed (keep your eyes closed throughout the entire meditation), notice how sound and then silence (or the lack of sound) come and go all by themselves, without us having to do anything – just allow yourself to become aware of this. Don't make a conscious effort to hear anything or to control what you hear. Just let the next sound come into your awareness and hold it gently there as long as it lasts; then be aware of the silence or the next sound that replaces it. Notice how you don't have to do anything to cause the sound to happen.

Now bring that same kind of open awareness to your own breath. Just notice how it happens; how each breath simply follows the next. Let your awareness rest there, with your breath, with the sensation of air entering and leaving your body at the tip of your nose. Don't try to force anything. Just breathe in and out through your nose as normal. You're breathing anyway, so just notice the breath that's there.

Now expand your awareness to follow the cycle of the breath. Notice the air entering your nostrils, and follow it gently. Notice your chest expanding, then your belly and the little pause before the process is reversed again. Don't try to take a special kind of breath, a deeper or shallower one – just allow it to happen, as you did when noticing the sounds around you, as follows:

In…

Out…

In…

Out…

Especially when you first begin this simple breath meditation, you'll find that your mind will wander, or even run amok, processing a seemingly never-ending stream of thoughts: *I must remember to make out that to-do list when I'm finished here*; feelings – boredom, frustration, happiness; and bodily sensations – being too hot, too cold, having an itch, or feeling various aches and pains in your body. This is OK – remember, we're training the mind. Every time your thoughts take off and try to pull your attention in many different directions, just gently and patiently bring your awareness and focus back to the breath.

Don't criticize or be harsh on yourself for becoming distracted. Instead, each time you bring your attention back to your breath, congratulate yourself! The practice of mindfulness lies in this simple exercise of gently bringing our awareness back to where we want it to be. That's all.

If you find at any point that you are concentrating overly on your breath, then just go back to noticing the sounds around you for a moment, and from that point of openness, gently bring your focus to your breath again and rest your awareness there once more. If you find that you're getting tired and sleepy, you can simply open your eyes for a few moments and gaze in an unfocused way at whatever is in front of you, or into the middle distance. This will break the stream of your thoughts. Then, close your eyes again and bring your attention once more to the breath.

When the 20 minutes, or the allotted time you have given yourself, is up, take some deeper breaths in and out of your nose, and bring your awareness once more to any sounds you can hear. Gently open your eyes and sit quietly, allowing yourself to slowly 'come back' to your surroundings. Allow yourself a few moments to reflect on your meditation and any realizations or insights it may have brought you.

⌣

When we focus our awareness on our breath as it enters the body, expands the chest and abdomen and then leaves the lungs again, we are bringing mind and body together. These two constituent parts of our being cannot exist without one another, and naturally exist as one. When we bring mind and body together, it is our most natural and favourable state and as such, we become at once highly focused and deeply relaxed. Even as you increase and develop your meditation practice, you will find that the Meditation on the Breath is one of the most important in terms of heightening your perception and deepening your awareness. Your time spent meditating will become something you look forward to and something you enjoy.

If you are new to or coming back to meditation practice after a long break, please be gentle with yourself. When you catch your mind wandering, give yourself credit. Acknowledge that the majority of the time, you will wander down the rabbit hole of thought without even realizing it, but that this time you haven't. If you look at it this way, the mind can never wander too much because every time it does is just another opportunity to practise bringing it back again.

When practising a meditation that uses a focus object, as in this case the breath, it's important to note that when you are aware of anything other than your focus object that thing is a distraction and means your mind has wandered. Thoughts like, *I'm not doing this right* or *I need to focus more* might seem relevant, but they are just thoughts. The same goes for images that might form in your mind's eye or feelings, like irritation and impatience. When you experience anything other than an awareness of your focus object (breath) simply recognize it for what it is – a distraction – and bring your attention back.

You might also choose to record the meditations in this book before using them so you can just close your eyes and rest into the moment.

Finally, however hard this may be, it's important not to have any expectations for your meditation – no goals. I know that some people have a hard time with the idea of having no purpose to their meditation and I frequently get asked, 'What's the point of doing it, if there is no goal or clear objective?'

In reply to this question, I often point out the fact that many people habitually go for a walk with no intention of going somewhere in particular to do something specific – they just go for a walk. Meditation is like that too – you're just meditating. In Zen, they have a wonderful word for this: *zazen* – which means 'just sitting'. So, let your formal meditation be that – simply sitting, and nothing else.

———

Chapter 4

Heightening your Focus: Targeted Meditations

*'Meditation can help us embrace our
worries, our fear, our anger; and that
is very healing. We let our own natural
capacity of healing do the work.'*

THICH NHAT HANH

In this chapter, I would like to look at a few more simple meditations which you can use as part of your twice-daily formal mindfulness practice sessions. These are just a few of the most basic, and most important, meditations – once you have mastered them, you will find any number of others on some of the great mindfulness resource websites/apps to be found online.

Some websites I can recommend are www.headspace.com and www.mindful.org; you will find some really appealing meditations for kids on www.annakaharris.com. In terms of the various apps available, I really like *Stop, Breathe & Think* (SBT), which starts by gauging your current mood and uses this as a basis for recommending a mindful meditation tailored to help. *Simple Habit*, *Aura*, and *Mindful* are great apps that will send you meditation reminders once you've programmed in a time of your choosing for meditation. They also provide you with 'mindful moment reminders' throughout the day, by way of notifications, which invite you to bring your full awareness to the present moment at random times during your daily activities.

Before starting with some more basic meditations, I want to stress again the importance of establishing a routine in your formal mindfulness practice, and sticking to it. As discussed in the last chapter, we are now engaged in the process of retraining our minds – and like any process of retraining, this is something which requires time, commitment and above all, regular practice. Only by regular formal practice and the effort to consciously bring the same quality of mindful attention into our daily lives, will we truly be able to live mindfully, and gain access to the higher levels of awareness this allows.

Meditation on the Body

I'd like to now look at another key foundation practice, **Meditation on the Body**, which follows on from Meditation on the Breath, which we looked at in the last chapter. As with Meditation on the Breath, this also uses a point of focus – the body – as an anchor for our awareness, i.e. something to bring the mind back to when it starts to wander (which, especially at first, it inevitably will). As with our breath, the body is always available to us, no matter where we are or what situation we find ourselves in. Each time we lose focus and begin to find ourselves ruminating on anything other than what is happening precisely in the moment, we can gently bring our attention and awareness back to the body, and the physical sensations we are feeling in the present. As well as enabling us to heighten our focus and practise bringing our minds back again and again to the present, this meditation also enhances the ease with which we can connect with the immediate sensations in our bodies – something which, as we will discuss in Chapter 9, and will ultimately enable us to have greater control over our actions and responses or reactions in any single moment.

Meditation on the Body is best done standing up – however, especially initially, you can practise sitting down if it's more comfortable.

Now stand up, with arms by your sides and your feet shoulder-width apart.

Take a deep breath and release it slowly, always in and out through your nose. And again, breathe in through your nose and then out through your nose. One last time, and this time as you slowly release your breath, just relax your body and allow your eyes to soft focus on the space in front of you.

Bring your attention to the top of your head and feel whatever sensations are there. Slowly let your awareness move downwards, to your forehead, then your eyes – cheeks – jaws – mouth – lips – and chin. What sensations do you find here, in each part of your body – heat, coldness, tension? If there are no sensations, just note that and move on.

Now move your focus down to the sides of your head, and notice any sensations around your ears, then your neck and throat. Feel your shoulders, become aware of any tension that may be in them, and slowly move your awareness down your upper arms – then your elbows, wrists and hands, front and back. Feel your fingers, and, for example, the sensation of your fingers and thumbs touching the fabric of your clothing.

Bring your focus back to your neck and throat, then the inside of the throat – what sensations are there? Move your attention down through the chest, the ribcage – maybe you can feel the sensation of the air there as you breathe in and out? And then move your focus on to your abdomen.

You are not looking for anything in particular – any specific sensation, pleasant, unpleasant or neutral – you are just noticing whatever feelings you find as you move your awareness down your body, noting whatever sensations arise into your awareness without trying to judge or categorize them. Whenever your mind wanders – to thoughts of a past event, your plans for tomorrow or any other such distraction – just gently bring your attention back to whichever part of the body you were focusing on before you got distracted.

Now bring your attention back to your neck once again and slowly down your back. Simply be aware of whatever you feel in each successive part of your body. Settle into the feelings in the area around your pelvis. Then slowly bring your awareness to your thighs – and knees – and calves – down through your legs to your ankles. Move your focus to your feet now: first, the tops of your feet, and then, the soles.

Be aware of the sensation of each foot, in turn, making contact with the floor.

Now just become aware of the sensation of your body as a whole. Try to imagine your body, not as you usually do, but just as a mass of all the sensations you've brought your awareness to during this meditation. Simply let your attention be taken to whatever sensation takes precedence in this moment. Now let your awareness move around to whichever sensation is the strongest.

Next, slowly scan your entire body from top to bottom, from your head to your feet. If, as you scan, you come across areas of tension or pain, take a moment to just be aware of, and rest in, that sensation. Don't label it as bad or good. Just acknowledge its presence. Now try to imagine your next in-breath being guided directly to that part of your body. Breathe into that area. With each in-breath, imagine healing and relaxation going to the area in question – maybe as pure white light, for example. When the tension eases, just move on with your scan.

Once you have completed your scan, slowly open your eyes and take a few deep breaths, as you allow yourself to tune in once more to your surroundings and to come back to your day.

Open Awareness Meditation

The next meditation is in some ways a step on from the meditations on breath and body, in that we will no longer have an anchor to which we can constantly bring back our focus, should our minds begin to wander. For this reason, I would advise you to try it only once you have established the first two as a regular part of your daily practice, and as such, have developed your ability to focus to some degree. **Open Awareness Meditation** is an extremely beneficial one but, since there is no in-built anchor, it is also the easiest to get lost in, and find yourself being carried away by your thoughts in a completely different direction.

When we sit and meditate in open awareness, we simply observe whatever comes to our attention in any given moment. We will use three terms – 'thought', 'feeling' and 'sensation' to denote whatever mental formation has our attention. For example, if we become aware of a thought, such as *I must remember to get milk on the way home from work tonight*, we just silently say the word 'thought' to ourselves. If we become aware of a feeling – such as happiness, anxiety, anger, agitation, contentment, ease and so on – we simply acknowledge it by silently saying the word 'feeling' to ourselves. When a physical sensation comes to our attention – say, an ache, a pain or an itch, a sound or a smell – we just note that, and identify what it is, by saying the word 'sensation' to ourselves.

During this meditation, a key point to note is that whatever comes into your awareness at any given moment, don't try to immediately qualify or judge it – by labelling it as good or bad, reprehensible or praiseworthy, right or wrong, and so on. For example, don't label a happy thought as 'good' or a painful sensation as 'bad'; don't classify a feeling of anger as 'justified' or 'inappropriate' and so on. Simply note, and neutrally acknowledge, whatever takes your awareness by using one of the three terms: thought–feeling–sensation.

During this meditation, try not to allow your attention to get caught up in or stuck on one particular thought, feeling or sensation. When you become aware of a thought or feeling or sensation, just notice it as it arises, stays around for a bit and then leaves your awareness again, to be replaced with something else. Don't try to hang onto any one thing you become aware of, even if it makes you feel good. In the same way, try not to resist anything which comes to your awareness, even if it is unpleasant and makes you feel bad. Just note everything as it naturally arises, allowing one thing to be replaced by the next in the flow of your awareness.

Sit with your back straight and allow your eyes to close gently. To stabilize your mind and relax your body, start by focusing your awareness for a few moments on your breath as it passes in and out through your nostrils. Note this as a 'sensation'.

Continue this process, gently noting whatever you are aware of moment to moment – the thought which arises right now, the sensation which claims your attention in this moment, the feeling which makes itself known. As with the other meditations:

Whenever you find your thoughts taking you in another direction, do not regard this as a failure of some sort, or be harsh or impatient with yourself. Rather, congratulate yourself each time you are able to gently bring your focus to the present moment and simply note, 'thought'.

Retraining the mind takes time – it's been working in a particular way for many years, after all, so patience is required. You are going to need as much practice as you can get in bringing your mind back to your meditation, and so, each time you have to do so, it is something to be pleased about – yet another opportunity you've been able to use for positive benefit to yourself!

As I mentioned above, this Open Awareness Meditation is very beneficial. While of course all our time spent in formal mindful meditation is beneficial, this particular form of meditation benefits us in a very specific way. When we sit in open awareness, we bring our attention to the never-ending stream of 'stuff' that flows through our consciousness, in the form of thought processes – like ruminating, planning, obsessing – and feelings and physical sensations. In essence, we get the chance to watch the process of awareness. In doing so, we see how most of our mental effort is taken up with thought contemplating itself, in an endless – and mostly pointless – loop. This realization is incredibly freeing, because usually we put so much emphasis on paying attention to our mental chatter, and end up being pushed and pulled around by our thoughts and feelings.

In Open Awareness Meditation, we get the opportunity to see how transient our thoughts and feelings are, and how quickly they pass through our consciousness – if we allow them to, that is. We also get to experience in a very real way the surprising and sometimes startling fact about our thoughts

– that they are entirely of our own creation, that we make them up, and that they have no independent existence or reality of their own. With this realization, comes another – that if we create or make up our thoughts, then the feelings we experience based on those thoughts are also entirely of our own making. When we truly 'know' this, we can give up the notion that our feelings are somehow imposed on us by other people or situations. We see that they are of our own making and that, as such, we can change our feelings or simply not allow them to translate into actions or reactions.

Zen Meditation

This is one of my favourite mindful meditations and comes from the Zen tradition. As with most things Zen, there is a slightly different approach involved. **Zen Meditation** involves different pairs of words or phrases, or couplets. The first one is used on the in-breath and the second is used on the out-breath, and each couplet is repeated three times.

So, let's take the word pairing, 'deep, slow'. Deep is used on the in-breath and slow is used on the out-breath. Before you start this couplet, you can say to yourself, 'Breathing in, I breathe deeply; breathing out, I breathe slowly.' You then practise this. On the in-breath, breathe deeply, while silently saying to yourself 'deeply', and on the out-breath, release the breath slowly, while silently saying to yourself 'slowly'. Repeat this process three times for each pair of words.

Here are some more couplets for you to try:

~ **Calm, smile:** Breathing in, I feel calm; breathing out, I smile.

~ **Present moment, wonderful moment:** Breathing in, I am aware of the present moment; breathing out, I know it's a wonderful moment.

~ **Aware of body, relaxing body:** Breathing in, I become aware of my whole body; breathing out, I relax my body.

~ **Calm body, love body:** Breathing in, I calm my body; breathing out, I feel love for my body.

~ **Smile, release tension:** Breathing in, I smile; breathing out, I release tension from my body and my mind.

~ **Feel joy, feel peace:** Breathing in, I bring the feeling of joy; breathing out, I feel peace.

~ **As a flower, feeling fresh:** Breathing in, I feel as a flower; breathing out, I feel fresh and light.

~ **As a mountain, feeling solid:** Breathing in, I feel as a mountain; breathing out, I feel solid.

As you breathe in and out, try to notice the changes happening in your mind and body. For instance, as you breathe in and smile, and breathe out and release tension, can you feel the effect of smiling on your mind? Can you feel the change in your body as you release tension and become more relaxed?

Non-reactive Meditation

As we continue our practice of mindful meditation, we can begin the work of consciously expanding our awareness. We will soon start to realize that we can develop awareness of everything we experience, and our responses to what we experience – even those responses and reactions we tend to think of as automatic or involuntary, as being beyond our conscious control. **Non-reactive Meditation** shows us just that, while also allowing us to practise slowing down our reactions, and so gaining greater control over our minds and bodies.

When we sit in meditation, even after practising for some time, we will find that we often have a tendency to move, or fidget, and that we are not always aware we are doing it. If we move to scratch an itch, and someone asks why we just did this, we are liable to say that it was just an automatic, or involuntary, reaction. But is this true?

All of our physical movements are responses to either a stimulus from our senses – an itch causes a movement to scratch, a noise causes a movement of our head in the direction of the noise, and so on – or a stimulus from the mind – a thought, *Did I leave the oven on?* leads to the physical movement of going to check. So, stimuli send a signal to the brain, and the mind reacts with an action or movement which to us so often appears to be involuntary and something we have no choice in, and no control over.

However, once we know about the relationship between stimulus–mind–movement, we can watch it at work. We can become aware of the process. And once we are aware of it, we can make decisions at any point which bring the whole process under our conscious control to a far greater degree. So, with this awareness, we might decide not to move to scratch an itch and just to let it pass.

Begin by sitting on a chair or cushion with your back straight, and bring your attention to your breath or the sounds around you.

Once your body and mind are relaxed, make a determination to sit completely still, not moving a single muscle. Whenever an urge to move arises – for whatever reason – ignore it, and remain focused on sitting completely still. For a few minutes, just notice the impulses to move that come to your awareness and not acting on them.

Now, practise acting on these impulse in a voluntary, controlled way. (This is the opposite of the involuntary *rea*ctions we normally experience.) The next time you feel the impulse to move, just mentally note it. Then, only once you've done this, decide whether or not you are going to move. If you do decide to move, be aware of the whole process of that movement. For example, you might become aware of a pain or a feeling of discomfort in your leg. Make a mental note of this: *My leg is uncomfortable.* Now decide whether you are going to sit and examine the feeling of discomfort until it passes, or whether you will move your leg to a more comfortable position. If you decide on the latter, bring your attention to every part of the movement: the shifting of your weight to unfold your leg; the sensation of the movement of your leg at the knee as you stretch it out;

the sensation of your leg moving, as you reposition it in a more comfortable way. And finally, the resting of the body back into stillness.

Repeat this process for whatever stimuli/impulses arise during your meditation. You will probably find there are quite a few!

———

This meditation is really helpful for two reasons. First, it enables us to break or get out of the habit of automatically reacting to physical distractions during our sitting meditation and demonstrates in a very real way the power we have when we apply mindful volition. On a deeper level, applied over time, this practice trains the mind and body to be less reactive, by making us pay attention to, but not follow through on, those impulses we might previously have considered to be involuntary. We might also come to the realization that if we don't have to react immediately to physical sensations, then the same is probably true for our thoughts and feelings. That, if we bring awareness to thoughts and feelings we get to choose how to act on them and not blindly *re*act.

Allow your practice to develop

Now you have some basic but effective tools to help you begin your formal mindful meditation practice, and to start the journey of gently retraining your mind. Choose one of the meditations above and use that in your twice-daily sittings; when you get familiar with that one, just move on to another. No one is *better* than the others, and each will help you develop your awareness in different ways.

Lastly, and once more, always remember to congratulate yourself when you realize your mind has wandered and as you make the effort to bring yourself back to the meditation.

Please don't concern yourself with whether you are doing it 'right' or not. Your practice will develop at its own pace. Some days you might feel as though you are having an incredible breakthrough and others you may feel more like you are having a breakdown. At times you may feel bored and at other times energized and connected. This is all perfectly normal. The important thing is to set your routine and stick to it – no matter what.

If you are taking the time to meditate, you are doing it right.

Chapter 5

Bringing Awareness
into Daily Life

*'The moment one gives close attention to anything,
even a blade of grass, it becomes a mysterious,
awesome, indescribably magnificent world in itself.'*
Henry Miller

By committing to and engaging in a daily formal meditation practice, you have taken the first steps on the path to greater awareness. Soon you will start to see how putting this simple measure in place will bring a different quality to the way you perceive the world and your experiences of it. Such positive knock-on effects of regular meditation will however be even more powerful and wide-ranging if you are able to carry the same quality of focused awareness over into your everyday activities and routines. In other words, making the effort to regularly bring an attitude of mindfulness into the rest of your day – i.e. the time outside of formal practice – will serve to reinforce and consolidate all the benefits of that practice. This brings us to the second element of the work of developing greater awareness – that is, the effort to consciously integrate mindfulness into our everyday lives.

The monks of Plum Village

During my stays in Plum Village, Thich Nhat Hanh's retreat community near Bordeaux in France, I have had the opportunity to see first-hand how the Buddhist monks living there practise this second aspect of mindfulness. They do so in a very intense and focused way – something which always makes a deep impression on me whenever I spend time in their presence.

These monks live in groups of four, in very basic accommodation; each group is generally made up of two 'beginner' or novice monks, one monk of several years' practice (or what I sometimes refer to as a 'middle-y' monk), and one senior monk. While in Plum Village, I remember having a conversation with a junior monk during one of the communal mealtimes. After some introductions – it turned out that he was Irish too, and from Cork – he confided in me that he wasn't having a good day. When I asked why, he recounted how the morning had begun with him being gently but firmly chastised by one of the senior monks in his group, not long after he'd joined the others for breakfast.

'He told me that I hadn't opened the door mindfully. I hadn't walked to the table mindfully; I hadn't sat down mindfully, and I hadn't sipped my tea mindfully. And I had to concede that he was absolutely right. Let's just say, it wasn't the best start to today.'

Which goes to show that even Buddhist monks can have 'one of those days' now and again... As I said in Chapter 2, learning to live with awareness is an ongoing, lifelong learning process!

Everyday mindfulness

Of course, the monks in permanent residence in Plum Village have committed their lives to the practice of mindfulness and endeavour to focus all their energies single-mindedly on the development of awareness. So, such intense diligence on their part in these matters is only to be expected, of course – I'm not advocating that all of us should become Buddhist monks in order to attain a greater level of awareness. But there is certainly something important to be learned from their approach, and which we can adapt to our own lifestyles, circumstances and priorities.

The idea is to be 100 per cent present in whatever you are doing at any given moment – and in doing this, you will reclaim the present and reset the old, tired pathways of your habitual thoughts and experience every moment as something new and fresh. As we have seen earlier, mindfulness is a gentle retraining of the mind which enables you to break free from limiting beliefs and old, conditioned ways of seeing the world, and to establish a new sense of perspective on life. Formal meditation practice begins the process of retraining; bringing mindfulness into your daily activities is a way of continuing that retraining, until bit by bit, it becomes second nature and your way of being.

A lot has already been written about the various ways of bringing mindfulness into everyday life, and so I will just run quickly through some of the ones I, and the people I have worked with, have found to be the most effective. One important point to note here at the outset is that introducing a different quality into your daily life in this way doesn't involve interrupting or stopping what you are doing in any given moment in order to suddenly cut off and 'become mindful'. What it entails, rather, is bringing your attention back to your breath (*see Meditation on the Breath in Chapter 3*) and to what you are directly experiencing just then, physically and mentally – i.e., to the immediate sensations and feelings which come with the activity you are engaging in. In other words:

Focusing more intently on what you are doing and bringing your full attention to the present moment.

Don't bring anyone else into the shower with you

Aside from your 20 minutes of formal sitting, it's good to try to begin your day with some time when you consciously focus your full attention on what is happening right now. If, for example, you have a shower first thing, you could decide that you will keep your focus on the physical sensations of this usually pleasurable experience. Enjoy the freshness of the water – warm, lukewarm or cold – on your face and the rest of your body: your back, your arms, your legs, and down to the soles of your feet. Take in the smell of the soap or shower gel, and the sensation of your sponge, face cloth or loofah on your skin. Feel the water running over your head and smell the rich lather of shampoo as you massage it into your hair.

Each time you find your thoughts drifting – or returning obsessively – to the events, challenges and anxieties of the day ahead, try to bring yourself back gently to the physical sensations of showering. Decide that, for once, there will be no one else in the shower with you – that is, no one else occupying your thoughts and mental space, and preventing you from enjoying this personal morning ritual: not the work colleagues who will be with you in the team meeting that morning, or the client you have to meet later for a coffee, or the guy with a nasty bout of road rage who cut you up on the drive home from work yesterday. After all, rehearsing or reliving any of these things in your mind won't make the slightest bit of difference to the actual events, whether they are in the past or in the future. Allowing your mind to wander to them will just needlessly rob you of any pleasure to be had in the present moment.

Relying on the kindness of strangers

When you are on your way to work, or driving your kids to school, or generally out and about in the car, and find yourself sitting in traffic or stopped at traffic lights, take a few moments to focus your attention inwardly, and register what you are thinking and feeling. Then bring your attention to any physical sensations – your hands on the steering wheel, or on the handbrake or gear stick; your feet on the clutch and brake. If it's practical, and safe, close your eyes so as to heighten your focus on these sensations. And don't worry about missing the lights – some kind soul sitting in the queue behind you will be only too delighted to let you know when it's time to move on!

If you are standing waiting in line – at the bank, at the water cooler at work, at the cafe till when paying for your morning coffee – practise the Open Awareness Meditation outlined in the last chapter. Focus on your immediate feelings, thoughts and sensations, instead of getting stressed and staring with intent at the back of the person standing in line in front of you, or the lucky person who's at the counter now, and being inconsiderate enough to be exchanging a few pleasantries with the person who is serving. Willing the line to move more quickly won't make it happen, just as worrying unproductively about what's going to happen later that day won't in that moment make any difference to the result.

Once more, with feeling

At various intervals throughout your day, when the occasion arises, try practising mindful gratitude. When thanking someone for something they've just done – giving you your change at the counter, placing your purchases into a bag, bringing the coffee you ordered to your table, holding the door open for you, and so on – give your full attention to the act of thanking that person. Sometimes it can help if you make the effort to specify what you're thanking them for, i.e., 'Thank you for my tea', 'Thanks for my change', 'Thanks for packing my shopping', and so on. This focuses your attention on what's happening at that moment, as well as enhancing the quality of your interactions with the people you encounter during your day.

Feel the weight

If you work in an office or drive for a living, say, here's a great way to bring lots of mindful moments to your day. Every time you sit down – at your desk, or behind the wheel – just bring your attention to the sensation of weight where your bottom meets the seat. This takes no time and you probably sit down dozens of times a day. You might want to put a sticky-note reminder on your desk or dashboard to remind you – perhaps something like, 'Feel the weight.' Try to think of other actions you repeat throughout the course of your day that you can turn into mindful moments in this way – opening a door, for instance, picking up the phone to make a call, turning on the kettle, and so on.

Not talking with your mouth full

Now for perhaps one of the most important and beneficial ways of bringing mindfulness into your daily life – try eating your food mindfully. At mealtimes, eat slowly, chewing your food fully, and really savouring the aromas and tastes as you do so. Switch off all your devices, and don't bring your phone or tablet to the table with you; don't read the paper or allow yourself to go off into a reverie of worry about what's happening later that day or evening. If you are eating with others, focus on their conversation, while also keeping some of your attention on what you are eating. Try not to talk non-stop while you are eating – just focus on enjoying your food.

What you'll find is that you will enjoy your food so much more, as you'll be aware of what you are eating and of when you've had enough. You'll also be more able to stop before you're uncomfortably full. While you may eat less, you will feel more satisfied and replenished, because you've actually taken the time to enjoy the experience of eating and the flavour of your food in a more relaxed way. You also might be surprised to discover that some of the foods you eat regularly may not be as tasty as you thought, once you actually focus on really tasting them!

False busyness

All of this reminds me of an incident which happened a few years ago, when I'd been asked to join some people for dinner at a very expensive restaurant. This was the type of establishment I wouldn't normally frequent, so I was really looking forwards to going there, especially as it had a reputation for fantastic food. We were meeting to talk about introducing mindfulness into schools and, as this is something I'm passionate about, I knew I wouldn't feel out of place and that I'd have something to contribute.

On the evening in question, I duly arrived and took my seat at the table with the six other invited guests. We ordered our food, and after a short while our dinner was brought to the table – and the food really lived up to the restaurant's reputation: it was delicious! During the meal however, I noticed that none of my fellow diners in the group seemed to be paying any attention to their food. Two had laptops open on the table in front of them and were busy adding points to a discussion document; everyone else was talking non-stop.

About an hour later, we'd finished our food, our plates had been cleared away and we had begun discussing in earnest the detail of introducing mindfulness into schools. It was at this point that it occurred to me to try a simple experiment. With the discussion in full flow, I intervened to ask a very straightforward question of my fellow diners: 'Can you name four foods that were on your plate for dinner?' Of the six, only two could remember what they'd actually eaten!

To me, this seemed like such a shame. Someone had gone to great care to prepare our meals, someone else had gone to great expense to provide a beautiful environment in which we could eat, and the waiting staff had gone to great trouble to make sure we each had everything we could possibly want to be able to enjoy our food. Yet, an hour later, most of our group couldn't even recall what had been on their plates, let alone what it tasted like! The truth was that nothing very beneficial had come from all the multitasking over dinner – the intense conversation, the frantic work being done on laptops, everyone talking over each other without listening to what any one person was saying. There hadn't been any really productive exchange at all – and over and above this, all the activity had served only to deny our group the pleasure of enjoying what was in front of us. It would have been far better if we'd decided to keep all the serious chat until after the meal, and simply focused for the time being on the delicious food and each other's company. I have no doubt that conversation and the exchange afterwards would have been far more creative. But if we'd done that, we might not have looked so industrious and important to the outside world of course!

This is exactly the sort of 'false busyness' a lot of us feel the need to involve ourselves in on a daily basis. Wouldn't life be a lot more agreeable, and far more productive too, if we gave this up and just allowed ourselves to enjoy the present moment?

'Do your dishes before you change the world.'
THICH NHAT HANH

There are all sorts of daily tasks that you can resolve to give your full, undivided attention, as a way of bringing a quality of mindfulness to 'ordinary', everyday life. In Buddhist monasteries, the resident monks and those who are there on retreat are encouraged to approach these small chores – basic activities which people all over the world must engage in routinely, such as preparing and cooking food, sweeping the floor, washing the dishes, making the bed, cleaning the bathroom – with the same kind of focus and concentration as they bring to formal meditation.

The idea is that there is a joy and simple pleasure to be had in doing these everyday things with care and attention, if we don't allow our usual mental chatter to distract our focus; if we're not hurrying and constantly anticipating the next, 'more important' thing in our day. The underlying truth is that these small things are just as important in our lives as anything else; that it is not the activity we are engaged in that defines its importance, but rather the quality of attention, and the degree of care, we bring to it.

Something special happens when we are able to give this quality of attention to the things we do – even the simplest daily tasks and chores. Back to my stay at Plum Village, and a scene which I still think back to now.

In sight of mindfulness

It was mid-morning on a beautiful summer's day, and we'd not long finished the communal breakfast. Our retreat group had been assigned to kitchen duties that day, and we had just finished clearing the breakfast dishes and cleaning and sweeping the dining area – a few of us were standing outside in the sunshine for a brief moment, now that our work was done. Meanwhile some of the resident monks were gathering a group of retreat visitors together in preparation for Walking Meditation through the beautiful orchards and woods of the village. There was an atmosphere of restfulness and tranquillity, as there always is in Plum Village. All of a sudden, a huge, dazzlingly white, brand-new 4×4 swept into the forecourt in front of the kitchen area where we were standing. It was a slightly startling sight, since cars and other vehicles are always left in one of the discreet car parking areas well away from the village. The driver had obviously taken the wrong turn – or was simply ignoring the usual etiquette.

We all watched wordlessly as the vehicle came to an abrupt halt. The doors were thrust open and out stepped, from the front, a middle-aged couple and, from the back, two gangly, sullen-looking teenage boys. All four stood there, glaring around them in a slightly indignant fashion.

As the father fired a series of terse questions at us in a clipped Canadian accent – 'Is this Plum Village? Where are you supposed to park? Is there an ATM nearby?' – my attention was drawn to the older of the two boys. He was dressed from head to toe in pristine, bright-white, Fred Perry monogrammed sports gear – shorts, polo shirt and sports shoes – and weighed down with an array of the latest electronic devices only the wealthiest of teenagers could afford to own at the time: iPhone, tablet, headphones and so on. When he finally managed to tear his eyes away from the screen of his phone, he looked around him, and at us, with utter disinterest – it was clear that this was the last place on Earth he wanted to be. I couldn't help thinking how completely out of place he looked against the backdrop of Plum Village, with its simple, modest dwellings and community outhouse buildings, the small groups of resident monks in their muted brown robes, the utilitarian, pared-down style of dress of those on retreat like myself, and the quiet, slightly swaying tranquillity of the trees behind us.

Just at that moment, some distance away, one of the monks, Brother John (not his real name), appeared from his monastic hut – he was heading to join the group who were assembling for Walking Meditation. Glancing up from his iPhone again, the sulky Canadian teenager caught sight of him – and suddenly, he was transfixed. Like all the resident monks in Plum Village, Brother John was walking with that special quality of attention unique to those who devote their lives to mindful living. The manner in which he took each step, serenely putting one foot in front of the other, was the very embodiment of the kind of focused awareness which only a devoted practitioner of mindfulness can achieve.

Thus, in the simple act of walking, Brother John – who, I have to say, hand-on-heart, was one of the grumpier of the resident monastics in the village at the time! – was an utterly compelling sight for this otherwise rather jaded teenager. For the few minutes that it took for John to reach the rest of the assembled group, the boy literally could not take his eyes off him, and simply stared in stunned silence, his mouth hanging open.

As we know, teenagers can be a tough crowd at the best of times. So the fact that this boy, who was more than likely a tougher audience than most, was completely mesmerized by the sight of a little Buddhist monk walking down a dirt path in a remote village in Bordeaux is a powerful gauge of the impact a mindful bearing can have!

The joy of living simply

Once we start to slow down and really engage with the small, mundane tasks which are the stuff of daily life, we begin to realize that a life pared down to the simplest activities, and indeed lived in the simplest of circumstances and surroundings, can be full of joy and peace. Although we might not all be able, or want, to live as Buddhist monks do, this is an important realization to have. It certainly helps us to re-evaluate how many of us seem compelled to live today – with an increasingly frenzied schedule of seemingly essential activities and events, which enables us to brag to others about how busy we are. The subtext being that because we are very busy, we must therefore also be very important.

Slowing down and finding simple pleasure in mundane, everyday tasks also gives us a new perspective on living our lives at the beck and call of the endless demands of social media on smartphones and tablets, Fitbits, apps and all the other 'techy' gadgets so many of us now regard as must-haves. In our modern world, it seems that being hopelessly overstretched in our time and resources – and complaining loudly about it – has become a badge of honour. Even within individual couples, many indulge in this 'competitive busyness', an endless game of one-upmanship in which the busiest, and most exhausted, person is seen as the 'winner'.

Three mindful breaths

Initially, it may not be easy to bring mindfulness into your day – naturally enough, as it takes some time to retrain the mind. The opposite of mindfulness is inattention or absent-mindedness, slipping into default mode, and while most of us find being mindful relatively easy if someone directs our attention to it and guides us through it, the problem is that as the day progresses, we tend to get so caught up in our haste, worry or stress that we forget all about trying to be mindful.

A helpful strategy, especially when you are just starting out, is to simply pause in what you are doing every so often and take three mindful breaths. You won't have to stop or interrupt whatever you're doing, but this simple tactic will help you to refocus, gather your thoughts and bring some calm to the present moment.

Using reminders, ancient and modern

Some people find it helpful, especially at first, to rely on technology to remind them to take some mindful time. There are some very useful apps now for your phone, or downloads for your PC, which can be set up so that an alert will sound every half hour, every hour or whatever regular intervals you determine throughout your day.

You could also use your phone in another way to help you be mindful. Decide that, every time a call comes in or you get a message alert, you are going to use this as your cue to bring awareness to your next three breaths. Only once you've done this, can you answer the phone or respond to the text or email as usual.

In relation to this, you might even want to take a tip from Buddhism and buy a small bowl bell and mallet (or 'bell inviter') for your home – in our house, we have a small, 25cm Ching bowl, but any bowl bell will do. The bell can be placed somewhere where there tends to be fairly frequent traffic, and also where the sound will be heard throughout the house – outside the bathroom on the stair landing, perhaps, or in the hallway. Every so often, as you or others pass the bell, you or they can ring it – or 'invite' the bell to sound, as we say in Buddhism – to remind everyone in the house to take a moment or two and bring back their awareness to the present. They and you don't necessarily have to stop what they or you are doing, but just become quiet and focus on the breath.

In our house the bell bowl is kept on the landing so anybody – including our two young sons – can randomly invite the bell to sound. When we hear the bell, we all stop what we are doing and concentrate deeply on our breathing until the reverberation has faded. Then we all say 'thank you' to whoever rang the bell. We thank this person because they have provided us with an opportunity to be mindful. Using the bell in this way has the obvious benefit of increasing our daily 'mindful moments'. In our case, it also allows the boys to be involved at some level in our family's practice, without the need for formal meditation.

Interestingly I know that in some families – and, I must admit, even in ours on the odd occasion – the bell has been used by the children of the house as a way of calming conflict. So if they hear mum and dad arguing, they will sound the bell – this encourages everyone to be quiet and take a few moments of calm reflection. The parents in such houses have told me that this gesture on the part of their children usually has the effect of making them come to their senses a bit. They realize that their kids are literally saying, 'Stop arguing now, you two!' – something which young children are not always able, or allowed, to do.

For me, in any case, Buddhism aside, the beautiful sound of a resonating bell bowl is a far more calming and serene way to be brought back to awareness than the electronic tones of an app or smartphone alarm. But each to his or her own, of course! Which brings me on to the key point that, in all of this, you should always choose the things which will work best with your own unique lifestyle and circumstances. If you are a technophobe, you'll hardly find it easy to download and programme an app for your phone. If you frequently have to take clients out for lunch, you may (wisely) decide that these won't be the best times to consciously choose not to speak, in order to focus 100 per cent on mindful eating. Be realistic – and creative – in determining what the most effective and workable approach for you as an individual will be.

Being flexible and creative when trying to incorporate mindfulness into your day can reap huge rewards: this is something I have witnessed first-hand since I began teaching mindfulness.

The mindfulness of 'mam'

A few years ago, I was contacted by a local medical doctor in our area (who is also a personal acquaintance), asking if I might be able to help one of his patients with some basic training in mindfulness.

The patient, Marie, was in her late 30s, was working part-time from home as well as looking after her five children – all boys and all under the age of nine. Marie was feeling constantly stressed and harassed; she was not sleeping and barely finding the time to eat properly; she was certainly getting very little time for herself, let alone a short break or even a day or two away from the boys occasionally. This situation had been ongoing for some years, and Marie's GP was concerned that she was on the verge of some kind of complete physical and emotional collapse. He had prescribed various anti-anxiety medications, as well as sleeping tablets and antidepressants but, he told me, these could only be short-term measures and weren't a healthy, or even a very effective, long-term solution. He was hoping that mindfulness might bring Marie some relief.

I agreed to meet Marie and said I'd do my best to help her. At our first appointment, when I mentioned formal meditation and that, ideally, she should devote 20 minutes morning and evening to its practice, she just stared at me as if I'd lost the run of myself completely! Although in my experience most people can manage to set aside 20 minutes twice daily if they apply themselves, in this case – given that Marie's youngest was usually up and about at around 5:30 a.m. – I knew better than to suggest that she set her alarm clock half-an-hour earlier. We agreed instead that she would do her formal practice only once daily, in the evening, once all the kids were in bed – if she could manage to stay awake that long, that is...

However, it was also clear that it was vital for Marie to try to reduce her stress levels during the day as well. I chatted with her about the possibility of getting an app for her phone, but she said that that might end up being a double-edged sword: the two oldest boys were technology-mad, and she knew they'd most likely keep dashing to her phone to stop the alert (and invariably get there before she did) – and that a fight over her phone would almost certainly ensue each time, making any chances of being mindful very slim indeed!

We puzzled for a while about how she could remind herself to take time out every now and again – even for three mindful breaths. All at once, Marie came up with an inspired suggestion: 'Why don't I use the word "Mam" as my trigger to do some mindful breathing?'

With five young boys clamouring for her attention the whole day long, I realized that this word was one which would be heard repeatedly in her household – probably almost non-stop at times, I imagined!

This strategy worked a treat. Every time one of the boys uttered the word 'Mam', Marie deliberately paused to bring her awareness to her next three breaths – and only then to attend to whatever the demand for her attention required.

At first, the boys were a little put out – why did their mother just seem to go quiet for a few moments and not immediately jump to attention the way she usually did every time they wanted her to do or look at something? Soon, however, they accepted this new state of affairs – and began to notice that their mother was much calmer and more relaxed than before. As the older boys put it, when chatting to me at one point, she was far less 'narky' and didn't 'give out' to them all the time any more, the way she used to.

When Marie went to her next doctor's appointment, just a few weeks later, he too could see a change in her. After four months, in which she stuck to this new approach with great determination, all her indicators for stress were significantly reduced. Her doctor was able to suggest that she start to gradually tail off the heavy-duty sedatives she'd been on for quite some time. She was also able to reduce her other medications to the lowest doses. Marie was, and continues to be, a real success story in terms of what mindfulness makes possible.

We practise mindfulness in order to live mindfully – and living mindfully brings a whole new, more positive quality to our daily existence. The more time we spend being aware of whatever we are engaged in, the less time our mind has to wander into default mode. Remember, the mind holds one thing at a time. The more mindful we are, the less time we spend in default-mode thinking. And the less time we spend in default mode, the less time we find ourselves being pushed and pulled around by thoughts we are unaware of, which in turn will generate feelings we don't want and cause us to act in ways we don't like.

Most people spend their days lost in regret, worry, thinking, planning and all the other ruminating activities of the mind, leaving little room to focus on *what is happening and what they are experiencing, right now.* So many of our everyday tasks and activities are done on autopilot, while our minds are off somewhere completely different – and most often, somewhere not very conducive to our wellbeing. This leaves no time to enjoy the present moment. Once you begin to bring the gentle attention of mindful awareness to your daily life, after even just a little time, you will find a sense of extraordinary joy and calm in the *ordinary* things you do every day.

As you make the effort to bring
mindful moments into your everyday
life, these moments will gradually
begin to merge – and before you
know it, you are living mindfully.

Walking Meditation

I want you to go for a walk! Right now, if you can. This will be a walk with a difference, because it a **Walking Meditation**, and I want you to notice that you are walking. Go outside – it doesn't matter if you're in the city, village or countryside – and start to walk. You're not going anywhere in particular; you're just walking.

As you walk, bring your attention and awareness to the movement of your legs. Notice how each knee bends backwards and how each foot leaves the ground. How the weight of your body then shifts to the opposite leg; how the heel of each foot makes contact with the beautiful planet we all live on. Feel the sensation of each foot in turn rolling forwards from heel to ball, and finally to the toes. Really focus on the detail of the sequence of movements involved in walking.

While doing this exercise, the most distracting sense is sight. So, soft-focus your eyes in front of you, and don't 'look' at anything in particular – just focus your main attention on the movement of your legs and feet. You don't have to walk really slowly for this, but you will find that your pace naturally slows down in any case.

Once you have mastered this focusing of your attention on the movement of walking, allow some of your awareness to go to the sounds that are around you. Most of your attention should still remain with the movement of your legs and feet – but just allow yourself to notice the sounds that come to your awareness, whatever they may be and for however long each one lasts.

Last, still primarily focusing on the movements of walking, allow some of your awareness to take in what you can see around you. Don't focus your attention on any one thing. Simply allow the sights to come and go, as you did with the sounds you could hear.

Practise walking like this as often as you can. Usually when we walk, our focus is totally in our heads. Worrying, planning, rushing, ruminating on past events. None of which will ever make the slightest bit of difference to events either in the future or in the past.

When we walk with full awareness of the movement of walking and what is happening around us (without getting distracted by thought), there is no room for worry – we are just walking. We don't need thoughts to walk, so why bother with them? Instead, enjoy the simple but profound pleasure of just walking.

Part III

PROFOUND AWARENESS

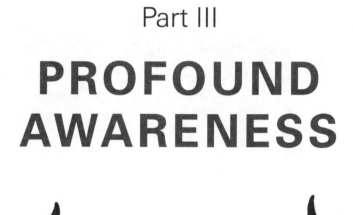

Chapter 6

Impermanence

'Anyone who has lost something they thought was theirs forever finally comes to realise that nothing really belongs to them.'
Paulo Coelho

In Arthur Miller's play *Death of a Salesman*, the main character, Willy Loman, talks about the impact that growing up without a father had on him: 'Dad left when I was such a baby, and I never had a chance to talk to him, and I still feel... kind of temporary about myself.' As a result of this feeling, Willy has thrown himself headlong into the pursuit of the American dream, and devoted his every waking moment to becoming the consummate salesman in the competitive consumer society of 1940s America, where success is defined as outdoing the people next door and being 'well-liked'.

But Willy is a complete failure as a salesman. His tragedy is that he is too deluded to acknowledge this, or the emptiness of the life he has chased after so relentlessly. At the end of the play, he sees suicide as the only possible course of action left to him and, sadly, this is one plan he follows through on.

While we may not all have had the misfortune to have been abandoned by a parent at a young age, there is surely something many of us can relate to in Willy Loman's deep-seated sense of insecurity. For Willy, this feeling of being 'kind of temporary', is something to be feared; it is the thing which has driven him to achieve, in the hope of gaining some kind of greater stability and sense of belonging.

If we are honest, many of us in Western society today feel the same. We know the reality of death is inescapable – and with it, the truth that we all really are only temporary fixtures in this life. Yet we seem to somehow believe that by owning more and more things – a bigger house, a newer car, more up-to-date technology – and by doing everything bigger and better than the rest of our peer group, we will feel more secure and more embedded in life. But the opposite is true.

One of the biggest benefits of practising mindfulness, and of the subtle shift in perception that this brings, is that we are able to live life more directly and see things as they really are. It becomes more difficult to live in a state of delusion and to buy into the fake messages and false promises of society – such as the one about getting and holding on to more stuff being the key to contentment. And undeniably, one of the most fundamental truths about life here on Earth is that nothing is permanent.

> There is absolutely nothing in this world that is everlasting and unchanging. I challenge you to think of something that is!

A parent's love

In my workshops, people don't always initially react well to the emphasis I put on the idea of impermanence. When I ask those in the room to give me examples of things they consider to be everlasting and unchanging, I will often feel a mood of resistance suddenly setting in. One of the most popular examples cited of something that is permanent is, 'my love for my children and my family'. When I respond by saying that no one's love for their children is absolutely unchanging or eternal, more than a few in the audience will usually react with indignation.

I suppose they think I am doubting the value of unconditional love – something which many of us who are parents like to think of as sacrosanct and believe we should strive to offer to our children. However, this is not the case: I am not questioning the value of such love or the aspiration to offer it. What I am simply saying is that the love we feel for our children, from moment to moment, is not always exactly the same. I might not feel the same sense of warmth and overwhelming love towards my three-year-old when he is trying to jam his toy car into our new DVD player, as I might on looking at his angelic, sleeping face when I check on him in his bed last thing at night.

Going 'past old'

This fact – that life is impermanent – is hardly a revelation, of course. Mere observation of the world and how it works provides us every day with proof of this truth. From the time in early childhood that we are first confronted with the fact of death, and are able in some way to take it on board – whether it be through the loss of a grandparent or other relative or even a beloved pet – it is clear to us that impermanence is one of the defining features of this world in which we live.

As with many other things, children are generally accepting of the reality of death, in ways which can seem matter-of-fact and devoid of the emotion or the drama often invested in it by us adults. After my mother died last year – the first experience my two young sons have had of losing a close relative – the younger, six-year-old Odhrán, came up with his own way of referring to the phenomenon of dying by telling people 'Nanny had gone past old.' To me, this showed that he was actually relating to this fact of life in a far more real way than many of us do as adults.

Somehow as we get older, the conditioning of society takes over and we distance ourselves from the truth of death. We say that someone 'bit the dust', that 'angels carried them away', that they were 'called home', that they 'entered the Pearly Gates', that they 'cashed in their chips' or 'passed away' – or we use one of many other countless euphemisms which are common currency in our language and betray our deep discomfort with the finality of dying. For many in our society, death is a taboo subject and certainly not the stuff of ordinary, everyday conversation – to talk about or dwell on it at any length is often quickly dismissed as 'morbid'. We surround it with ritual, we steep it in superstition and, most fundamentally, we invest it with fear. So much of human activity can be seen to have, at its root, the desire to somehow avoid or deny the reality of death – as idiotic as that sounds.

'Somehow, in the process of trying to deny that things are always changing, we lose our sense of the sacredness of life.'

PEMA CHÖDRÖN

While all of us are then at some level, from a very early stage, at ease with the transient nature of life, many of us have lost sight of this reality in our everyday lives and routines. This is where practising mindfulness and developing awareness can help us enormously.

At the most basic level, engaging in meditation allows each of us to see the ever-changing nature of our inner landscape. We become more aware of the continual shifting of thoughts and feelings; the way in which one thought gives way to another, and how one feeling or sensation always morphs into something else. The Open Awareness Meditation from Chapter 4 in particular brings us a heightened sense of the truth that, in our internal world – as in the external world – change is the only constant.

Ultimately, as we continue to practise mindfulness and strive to live mindfully to a greater and greater degree in our everyday lives, we will grasp the truth of impermanence in a far more profound sense. It is difficult to convey on paper or explain in words exactly how this feels or the impact this new level of awareness has on the way we see things. But once you know this truth on an absolute, instinctive level – in the same way that you know when you are hungry, or you know that you are in love – then you will understand what I am talking about, and be able to really feel how it changes so much. And if you continue to practise mindfulness and to live mindfully, there is no reason why you will not.

If all this sounds a little depressing or frightening or negative – and Willy Loman would definitely have thought so – I can assure you that it isn't. In fact, the very opposite is the case. Coming to grips with the truth of impermanence on a profound level is immensely liberating and something that will only lead to great joy. When you know that nothing, absolutely nothing, is forever, you are free to fully enjoy what is happening right now, without the fear that it will end (because you know it will); you can live without false expectations and be truly open to everything that is possible; you can ride out the rough times in the sure knowledge that 'this too shall pass'.

> *'If you suffer, it is not because things*
> *are impermanent. It is because you*
> *believe things are permanent.'*
> THICH NHAT HANH

As children, we seem able to take on board the reality of death, so there is a part of us then – the experiential self – which is profoundly 'knowing' of the impermanence of life. What lies at the heart of our suffering therefore is not the truth of impermanence, but rather our human tendency to want things to be otherwise. Wanting something to be permanent means that we try to hold on to it, we cling to it, we invest future hopes and expectations in it. When the inevitable happens and it proves to be temporary – as we likely knew all along it would – we experience the pain of dashed hopes, disappointed expectations, shattered dreams. This is suffering. But what drama and delusion there is in this suffering! If from the very outset we had just acknowledged, and kept to the forefront of our minds, the truth that nothing is permanent, all the drama and the futile suffering would not have had to be endured.

This isn't an easy concept to grasp, if you have never *known* it for yourself. To give you a sense of how denying the truth of impermanence can lead to suffering, let's consider a scenario we have probably all witnessed at one time or another – and may very well have lived personally.

Denise and John

One Friday, in the nightclub John goes to with friends every week, he spots Denise across the crowded bar. For him, it feels like love at first sight. She approaches, he catches her eye and it's not long before he's bought her a drink. The conversation flows and the chemistry fizzes. They go back to his house and she stays over. Over the following week, they meet up every day after work and spend every night together.

Three weeks later, things are still going strong. When John meets his best friend, Mark, for a catch-up, he tells him all about the new woman in his life.

'Mark, she's perfect for me in every way! She's gorgeous, really easy to talk to and best of all – she loves football! She's ambitious and I can tell she's really going places. This is it. I can't believe how right she is for me, and I can't believe I've only known her for three weeks... It's amazing and I really feel like she's "The One".'

'Well John, my friend, I'm really happy for you. I can hear wedding bells not too far away now. D'you think she wants kids as much as you do? You always said you wanted two boys and two girls, didn't you?'

'Yes, you could be right about the wedding bells. I think I'll have to move fast on this one – Jeez can't believe I just said that. I haven't mentioned kids to her – but you know what they are like anyway.'

After just three weeks, it's already clear that John has invested huge hopes in his new relationship with Denise, and that his expectations are sky high – to the extent that he can't possibly imagine *life without someone he has known for less than a month. He now regards Denise as a permanent fixture in his life, and feels a serious sense of ownership over her, her life and her future.*

This however is the point at which fear sets in.

That evening, after his chat with Mark, John calls Denise at home at 7 p.m. – as is now part of their daily routine, after their three short weeks together. Unusually, Denise's answering machine kicks in – she's not there. John leaves what he hopes is a nonchalant, breezy sounding message, asking her to call back as soon as she gets in. He tries her on her mobile, but it goes straight to voicemail: she must have switched it off.

For the next two hours, John sits by his phone, waiting for Denise to return his call. During those two hours, he goes through 50 shades of hell in his mind... First, there's mild annoyance – why didn't she tell him that morning that she was going to be out later? Soon, he feels downright angry – how dare she not let him know what her plans were? Where the hell could she be, anyway – they always talk around this time. Next, anxiety takes over: did something at work upset her, and has she gone for a drink to wind down from it? Or has something happened to Denise – has she had an accident, and could she now be lying unconscious somewhere in a hospital? No one would know to let him know, as he's not family or next-of-kin or anything. Yet.

Then John starts to feel an altogether different kind of fear... Maybe Denise has changed her mind about being with him? Did he do or say anything wrong the night before or that morning? Or perhaps she isn't as keen on him as he thought, and she hasn't had the guts to tell him to his face. Come to think of it, he's never had much luck with women – and maybe Denise is yet another one who's going to let him down, just like all the others. She is stunning and she could have any man she likes. THAT'S IT! She's gone off with someone else – someone from work? She did keep talking about the new guy who'd recently started in the front office. Yes, that must be it! She's probably with him right now, wining and dining with him, and flirting with him the same way she did with me.

All of this is John's personal suffering.

Sadly, this kind of scenario is all too familiar. Once we get emotionally attached, we tend to bring all our own fears and insecurities into the relationship with us, and it's not long before we begin to believe that person owes us an account of their every waking hour and even their every thought. And if we sense that in some way they are drifting away from us, slipping through our fingers emotionally or otherwise, our most common reaction is to grasp onto them and cling ever more intently. When we do this, it's almost inevitable that at some point, the other person will feel the strong urge to distance themselves from us. And so, ironically, clinging has had the opposite effect to that we'd intended.

How many marriages are fraught with such problems, arising from this skewed sense of ownership and from a fear of 'not being good enough'? To give a seemingly minor but nonetheless insidious example, we've all seen or heard of the wife who gives her husband a hard time because he stopped off on the way home for a quick drink after work (just the one), and didn't tell her beforehand. By the time he gets home, she's seething, even though nothing is really wrong and he's not even late for dinner. When taken to an extreme, this is the kind of thinking and reactive behaviour that can lead to the most appalling cases of domestic violence and abuse – the guy who regularly knocks seven bells out of his wife because, he imagines, she has looked at or talked to another man in a way which is disrespectful to him, her husband... And so, on it goes.

> *'If you look deeply into impermanence, you
> will do your best to make [your beloved]
> happy right now. Aware of impermanence,
> you become positive, loving and wise.'*
>
> THICH NHAT HANH

When we become aware on a profound level of the truth of impermanence, this brings a whole new sense of freedom, generosity and happiness to our relationships. The deep knowledge that our loved one is not, and never can be, a permanent fixture in our lives – because one day they will die, because they may change and one day decide to leave us, because they may be forced by circumstances to leave – liberates us from the unrealistic expectations which are at the root of our fears and insecurities. Facing, accepting and living every day with the awareness of the undeniable truth – that one day we will lose them – frees us from the limitations of fear and allows us to enjoy that person as fully as possible, right here and right now. And, just as clinging to someone produces the opposite effect, and ends up repelling them, the chances are that enjoying and loving someone fully in the moment makes it more likely that the relationship will succeed in the longer term.

Grief

When I talk in my workshops about the reality and the beauty of impermanence, another related issue around which some very strong feelings can, understandably, arise is that of bereavement. People will sometimes assume that my emphasis on impermanence implies a devaluing of human emotions and attachments, and, most powerfully, of the grief we experience on losing a loved one. Somehow the logic goes that, since I am highlighting the fact that emotions are transient, and people are finite beings, I must be suggesting that we should not set too much store by either one or the other, but instead see them for what they are (things of no lasting value), and from which we should remain emotionally detached.

This is not what I am saying at all, however. An awareness of impermanence does not mean that we should no longer feel emotions or attach value to people and relationships – quite the opposite is true. Knowing that everything is transient allows us to appreciate people and our emotional connections with them more than ever. Living with awareness means that we feel and experience everything differently – with an increased intensity, with a heightened clarity and with a purity which is free of our constant preoccupation with ourselves and our ego. And of course, beyond all of this, believing that only permanent things can have meaning is one of the great fallacies of our conventional way of seeing the world – a perspective which living with awareness will challenge at every cut and turn.

A sense of injustice versus a grief directly lived

Grief is something which we will all have to face to a greater or lesser degree at some point in our lives. The way in which we experience the loss of a loved one can be a powerful touchstone of the extent to which we are living in awareness.

I have of course had my own experiences of loss, and the grief that goes with it. Some years ago, within the space of a decade, I lost two brothers. This was at a time when I had not yet fully committed to practising mindfulness and developing awareness. Dan, the younger of the two, died at the age of 28, some 20 years ago. Ten years later, the older, Denny, died in his late 40s after a long illness. After each of these losses, I suffered prolonged, gut-wrenching grief. Then, last year, my beautiful mother, Rosie, died at the age of 80. Again, I mourned deeply for her – and continue to do so.

My experience of grief after the loss of my mother last year – by which time, I had been practising mindfulness for close to 11 years – was noticeably different to how I felt after the deaths of my brothers. Of course, every experience of grief is different *per se*, since each time we are grieving for a different person, who will represent something different to us because of who they were as an individual and how they related to us, and vice versa. It is also true that the person who suffers bereavement will be different each time, since in the interim, and with the passing of time, they will have changed and evolved in their own terms. The loss of a mother may feel different to the loss of a brother; grief will be experienced differently by someone in their 30s and someone in their 50s, and so on. However, when I say that my lived experience of grief before and after living with awareness was different, I am talking about some specific and profound distinctions which are not related to the nature of the relationship I had with each person, or the external circumstances in my own life at each point.

My grief for my brothers was very much coloured in both instances by the sense that something had been 'taken from me'. At times my predominant impression was that their loss was an injustice that had been inflicted on me, and about which my overriding feelings were anger and resentment, rather than a sadness more directly related to the fact that Dan and Denny were no longer with us. The grief I did feel, and how I expressed it, was often clouded and muddied by my own preconceptions – or those of other people – about what being bereaved *should* look or feel like, rather than being a direct expression of what I was actually feeling at the time. Although I wasn't conscious of it at the time, perhaps my internal monologue went something like this: *I've just lost my brother – this is how I'm supposed to be feeling and acting... So, I need to make sure that I'm being seen to do so.*

Since both Dan and Denny suffered greatly in the final phases of their lives, after some time passed, I was able to periodically acknowledge a sense of relief that neither had to endure such suffering any longer. But, especially at the beginning, this would be quickly overshadowed each time by my preoccupation with how their deaths were affecting *me* and *my* life. I don't think I was a particularly self-obsessed or selfish person – or not a great deal more than many other people, in any case. However, because I wasn't living with awareness, I was locked into my own narrow vision of the world, and experiencing everything through the filter of my own ego and expectations.

When my mother, Rosie, died, I was living with the truth of impermanence at the forefront of my awareness on a daily basis, and didn't perceive her death with the same sense of an injustice, of something having been done *to me*. A profound acceptance of the reality that my mother's life was finite, as all of our lives on this Earth are, meant I was liberated from the cage of my own narrow perspective, where everything that happens – and everyone in my life – only has meaning and relevance in terms of how it, or they, relates or relate directly to me. In that sense, my 'I' came into play to a far lesser degree, and I was no longer tempted to cling to the idea of Rosie as only *my* mother.

Living mindfully and with awareness also allowed the grief I felt for my mother to be very pure. Although she had gone and would no longer be in my life, there was no feeling that 'I' had lost anything, or something had been inflicted on *me*. There was also no sense, as there had been when each of my brothers died, that, as someone who was bereaved, I *should* be feeling or acting in a certain, prescribed way.

It was due to all of this that I was able to experience my grief directly, as something immeasurably more profound. I felt intense gratitude for a life shared; I felt immense love for Rosie, for someone who had always tried her best. There was also a deep sense of joy in the realization that my mother's suffering (at least in this life) was now at an end. I felt incredible sympathy and compassion for my father, who did feel that his wife and life partner had been taken from him and who saw no way to cope. At times, sadness flooded my every cell and my every thought. All this was felt directly, and with an intense awareness of every emotion and sensation and inflection of my grief. At no time was my very real sense of grief contaminated by anything else – then or now. It was, and continues to be, direct experience at its rawest; grief felt without the filters.

As you continue to live mindfully and grow in awareness, you will find that living directly, and relating to things as they really are, is a truer and far richer way of being, as opposed to seeing and feeling things through old filters or from a conditioned, conventional perspective. The simplest things of everyday life become fresh again, always changing and somehow always new.

Good news

While I have spent some time here addressing aspects of experience which many of us might regard as difficult and even painful – the reality of death, grief and its associated suffering – I want to close this chapter by emphasizing once more the incredible sense of joy and freedom that living with awareness and with a deep, ever-present knowledge of impermanence brings. Once you truly *know* this reality, so much fear dissipates. Indeed, asking someone with this level of awareness whether they are afraid of life's impermanence is like asking someone whether they are afraid of being hungry. (Of course, I am talking here from the context of our Western society, where the basic things we need for survival, such as food, are generally in plentiful supply.)

Good times can be enjoyed more fully and more joyfully, precisely because of the knowledge that they won't last, and bad times are not as difficult to endure, since they can be faced with the resilience which comes from the same *knowing* of impermanence. Things are no longer fixed, rigid or preordained; there is a new quality of ease when it comes to day-to-day living.

Once more, the wise and powerful words of Thich Nhat Hanh perfectly sum up the joy, freedom and wealth of possibilities which this kind of profound awareness opens up for us:

> *'Impermanence is good news. Without impermanence, nothing would be possible. With impermanence, every door is open for change. Impermanence is an instrument for our liberation.'*

Meditation on Impermanence

⌣

Sit down on a cushion or chair, and focus on your breathing for a few minutes to settle your mind in the present. Now shift your attention to wherever you sense the breath most – entering or leaving the nose, in the rising and falling of the chest. When thoughts interrupt, just gently bring your focus back to the breath.

Now bring your awareness to your body, allowing your attention to settle on whatever sensation is strongest at any moment. Now an itch, now a cramp, a breeze against the skin, a tight muscle in your leg. Just allow your awareness and attention to float around the body to wherever it is drawn.

Now just be aware of your body as a whole. Try to see it as a mass of sensations. And think about what your body is made of, its different parts – like skin, blood, bones, organs.

Then think about how each of these parts of the body is in turn made up of yet smaller parts – for example, cells. We know that these cells are constantly moving, changing, dying and renewing.

Even though we are sitting still, not moving, every minute, every second, every millisecond, there is constant change. Continual movement is taking place in every part of our body, even at the level of the smallest cell.

Now take that awareness outside of yourself, outside of the body, and see if you can sense that the same is true for the things around you. The cushion or chair you are sitting on, the floor, the walls, the ceiling – all the things in this room are also made up of tiny particles. These particles are changing, every second, every millisecond – always moving and changing.

What about the things outside of the room?

There are people, whose bodies are also at a very subtle level constantly shifting, changing, not staying the same – from one millisecond to the next. There are trees, mountains, buildings, houses, cars, roads, clouds – all changing, moment by moment. The sun, moon and stars, the sky – never the same, from one millisecond to the next. They are not static, even though they might look stable and everlasting. We know that they are constantly changing, gradually disintegrating – and eventually they will cease to exist. They are not going to be here forever. Everything has its end; everything is impermanent.

Spend a few minutes now thinking about the impermanent nature of some of the things you are attached to – people, possessions, circumstances, your job, your appearance.

How will each of these things appear 10 years from now?

How about 50 years from now?

Or 100 years from now?

Now see if you can begin to get a sense of the joy that comes from this realization, that everything is impermanent. Think for a moment about how this deep knowing of the truth of impermanence frees us from fear. For if we know the things or people we are attached to are impermanent, we will not be so afraid of losing them. We will be free to enjoy them without clinging, without fear.

Now think about how the fear of losing what we cherish prevents us from truly enjoying what we cherish, right here and right now. Spend a final few minutes pondering this truth – impermanence doesn't cause us suffering. Wanting things to be permanent, when they clearly aren't – this is what causes us suffering.

Before you finish, take a moment to bring your attention to any sounds that come to your awareness: noises outside the room, inside the room, the sound of your breathing. Allow your eyes to open gently and sit for a little while, before moving on with your day.

—

Chapter 7

Feeling Profoundly the Connectedness of Everything

*'We cannot live only for ourselves. A thousand
fibres connect us with our fellow men;
and among those fibres, as sympathetic
threads, our actions run as causes, and
they come back to us as effects.'*

HERMAN MELVILLE

Have you ever had the experience – generally in times of
deep peace and relaxation – of feeling part of something
bigger, even if just for a few fleeting moments? Perhaps
as a child, you were outside one afternoon in the height of
summer, lying on the grass in the back garden or in a field in
the countryside, looking up at the vast, cloudless sky above
you, and you felt happy, peaceful, utterly in harmony with
everything around you? Or maybe as an adult, walking in the

mountains as the sun was setting, and stopping to look at the view stretching out endlessly before you, and seeing the sky and land merge seamlessly on the distant horizon. Or on a quiet beach somewhere, lying in the sun and taking a moment to look out over a beautiful calm blue sea, observing the sunlight glittering on its surface and hearing the cry of distant seagulls?

Many of us have had such moments of all at once feeling profoundly at one with our surroundings and the rest of the natural world, when everything seems to stop for a short time and we have the sense of being just a tiny, but nonetheless necessary, element in a much bigger picture.

Even if you have never had such moments of deep awareness until now, I can assure you that once you start practising mindfulness, they will in time become familiar to you. As you persist in your daily formal practice and, alongside that, continue to bring a mindful attitude into your everyday life, you will find that these momentary glimpses become part of a much broader, more profound awareness. At the core of this awareness is a sense that we, as human beings, are not merely self-contained entities – each of us separate from one another and from all that is around us – but rather that we are part of the whole, intimately bound up with all of humanity and our environment, the Earth and indeed with the universe. This profound realization – that we as individuals are a constituent part of the whole, and that everything in this universe is somehow connected and bound up with everything else – will transform your perspective on life, as well as the way that you live, in a very real, concrete sense.

If you are completely new to mindfulness, you may feel that what I'm saying is all a bit vague and abstract; a bit 'woo-woo'. And it's very possible that, without mindfulness or spiritual awareness of some kind, these experiences of a cosmic connection of sorts are indeed becoming rarer for all of us.

A modern disconnect

The way we live today is certainly conducive to a growing sense of disconnection – with each other, with the world around us, with the true nature of life as it is. Very few of us now work or live in close proximity to the natural world, in the way the hunter-gatherers of our past did. We live in cities, perhaps in multi-storey buildings, we work in offices and travel in cars, trains or buses. Only those of us who make a conscious effort to do so have much contact with nature – perhaps by taking a walk at lunchtime in the limited green spaces (if there are any) close to where we work, or driving to the beach or countryside at the weekends.

Meanwhile our increasing dependence on IT and social media means that we can choose to function in our everyday lives with less and less immediate, physical contact with other people. We email work colleagues in the office rather than speaking to them; we can keep in touch with friends via text, Facebook or WhatsApp, rather than ringing them for a chat or meeting face-to-face. We carry our phones or tablets with us wherever we go, and our obsession with constantly checking them acts to further limit any *real contact* with others – a casual exchange with a stranger on our daily train commute, a friendly word with the person at the cash register in the local supermarket, or even – and very commonly – a decent conversation with our partners and children during family mealtimes (that is, if we even all still sit down together to eat at the end of the day). Who hasn't witnessed the depressing sight of a family with older children out for dinner together, where everyone is glued to their phones or tablets for the duration of the meal, and very few words are exchanged, other than placing the order and asking for the bill?!

We can now shop online and get home delivery, and so avoid going out of the house and having to interact with other people; we can pay bills and do all our banking online; we can get much of our entertainment online, with the result that outings to the cinema or theatre and so on are becoming rarer, and may soon even be a thing of the past. We can do a lot of our socializing online, with a whole younger generation now spending many hours of their free time alone in their bedrooms, playing games like Minecraft, Grand Theft Auto or Call of Duty. Admittedly they likely regard themselves as members of important online communities, and many lasting friendships are now made this way; however, because everything is done virtually, they might end up rarely going out of the house to physically meet with other friends. No wonder loneliness and a sense of social isolation have reached epidemic proportions in our society in recent years – not just among the elderly, but within the younger population too. The London *Telegraph* science section recently reported that: 'A recent study by the Mental Health Foundation found that 18–34-year-olds were likely to feel lonely more often than over-55s. Studies have shown that 20–80 per cent of adolescents report often feeling lonely, compared to 40–50 per cent of an elderly population.'[7] In January 2018, the UK government took the unprecedented step of appointing a Minister for Loneliness, as a measure to tackle the growing problem of social isolation.

All of these factors have combined to increase our sense of disconnection from each other, from our communities and the wider world around us, including of course our natural environment. This feeling of disconnect is only further emphasized by our modern tendency to live in our heads, analysing and over-thinking everything – from the implications of running to help someone else's child in a play park, to the possible repercussions of opening a door for a female colleague, or giving up your seat on the bus or the train for an elderly person or a pregnant mother with a toddler. And when you consider too that in our society, the individual is king, and we are encouraged, by an ethos of competition, one-upmanship and materialism, to look out for ourselves first and foremost, it becomes clear why our sense of alienation and isolation is potentially greater than ever before.

And yet most of us have an instinctive sense of the truth that we are all intimately, and necessarily, connected with each other and with the world around us. In the most basic sense, none of us lives in a vacuum, or would be capable of surviving for very long – let alone continuing to live our everyday lives in the way we are used to – if we suddenly found ourselves completely alone, without the assistance and contributions of other people, and our society as a whole.

A practical truth

For those who might feel that all of this is, as I said above, a little too 'woo-woo', I'd point out that even in the most concrete, practical way, the truth of our connectedness with each other is easily demonstrable. In relation to this, I remember a very simple exercise I did with our two young sons one time, when we were sitting at the dinner table.

Glass of water

Pointing to the glasses of water beside their plates, I asked them the question: 'Who do we need to be grateful to for this glass of water?' (We Buddhists put a very high value on gratitude and the importance of expressing it – and we like to remind our kids about this at every opportunity.) As usual, the boys entered into the spirit of things with great enthusiasm. In fact, their replies continued for so long that I began to wonder at one point if it had become just another delaying tactic on their part to avoid having to get ready for bed.

'Well, first of all you'd need to thank the clouds for raining and giving us the water – but before that, you'd need to thank the water for going up into the air as steam in the first place.' (I think the older one had just learned about evaporation in science that week in school.) 'Then you'd have to thank the universe for being here.'

We've got to the universe already, I was thinking, where can we go from here? But then the boys brought things back to Earth again very quickly: 'And after that, you'd have to thank the people who put down the pipes near our house, to help the water get to us... And then you'd thank their mams and dads, for having them in the first place. Oh, and then you'd have to be grateful to the man who built our house, and the people who taught him how to do that. And then you'd have to thank the people who built the road that the pipe runs besides, so that the men putting in the pipe could get to the right place. Then you'd have to thank the people who built the reservoir to collect the water and keep the water in, and the people who look after the reservoir and who clean the water – and you'd thank their mams and dads, and THEIR mams and dads before them, for having THEM... And then you'd have to be grateful to the lorry drivers for bringing the sand to make the concrete to use to put the pipes in. And their mams and dads... And then...'

As you can tell, this could have continued forever, for as long as the boys could think of who or what might possibly have any connection – no matter how tenuous – with the water and with it being available for us to drink. As I said, I was completely aware that it was a game for them, with a strong element of brotherly competition, which had quickly become just another way of putting off the evil moment of bedtime that evening. However, what it also showed was that they as young children had a basic understanding of a very important

truth: that every one of us is to a large degree dependent on
other people, and on our human community as a whole, even
just in living our everyday lives in the simplest ways.

Nothing comes from isolation

In reflecting further on the above example, where our interdependence on each other in a human community is clear, we can see another truth emerging – that nothing comes about in isolation; that for something to happen, a whole set of conditions must first be in place, and a lengthy chain of causes and effects set in motion. So we can see that not only are we as human beings interdependent and interrelated, but indeed that everything which exists and which happens in our world, and in the universe at large, is deeply interconnected.

The butterfly effect

Many of you will have heard of 'the butterfly effect', an expression coined by US mathematician and meteorologist Edward Norton Lorenz, which proposes that a butterfly flapping its wings in New Mexico can ultimately give rise to a hurricane in China. As far-fetched as this sounds, scientists have agreed that the connection is real (although it takes a very long time to trace the exact and complex chain of necessary causes and effects) – that, had the butterfly not flapped its wings at just the right point in time, the hurricane wouldn't have happened.

But thankfully we don't all need to be scientists or fractal mathematicians to 'get' this fundamental truth about our reality – that everything in the world, and in fact in the universe, is inextricably connected and bound up together.

Clouds and paper

In his recent teachings, Thich Nhat Hanh came up with a helpful way of expressing this, with the term 'inter-are'. Thus, he writes, everything – you, me, someone living in Timbuktu, my dog, your cat, the sky, the sun, the planet Venus and so on – 'inter-is'. He uses a rather poetic extended simile to sum this up, in a piece entitled *Clouds in Each Paper*:

> *'If you are a poet, you will see clearly that there is a cloud floating in this sheet of paper. Without a cloud, there will be no rain; without rain, the trees cannot grow; and without trees, we cannot make paper. The cloud is essential for the paper to exist. If the cloud is not here, the sheet of paper cannot be here either. So, we can say that the cloud and the paper "inter-are".'*

If all of this is getting a bit abstract and 'head-wrecking' (an expression I often use when I teach!) – and I understand of course if it is – I will ask you to just come back to the immediate here and now, and to trust your own deep intuition and knowledge about life. The next chance you get, simply look out of a window and gaze at the view. Take three slow, mindful breaths, as described in Chapter 5, and gently bring yourself fully into the present moment. Especially if you have already begun practising mindfulness, it is possible that after a while you may experience yourself as part of a continuum, part of everything around you, part of the natural world. You may lose your usual sense of any separate self. This is the wisdom of your own, direct experience. This is not philosophy, or science, or religion – it is what you instinctively know about the way life is.

In Buddhist teaching, a traditional metaphor for this insight – that, although we may think of ourselves as so many separate individuals, we are in fact all part of the whole – is that of waves in the sea. Although it is often used, it is nevertheless very effective and very beautiful.

Picture a vast expanse of ocean on a windy day, far away from land, where countless small, white-crested waves are visible on the choppy surface, constantly rising and falling through the force of the tide and the strength of the wind. In the absence of awareness, we tend to imagine that each of us is one of these tiny waves – individual, separate, making its way independently on its long journey to the shore, as we do as individuals in life. With deeper insight however, we realize that we are not separate at all, but that we are all one – just as single waves are part of the same vast body of water, which is the ocean, endlessly rising and falling, advancing and receding, ebbing and flowing. What we thought were separate elements, discrete entities with a beginning and an end, are all part of the same whole; each wave is intimately related to and affected by every other one, just as we human beings are in life. The wave cannot be separated from the ocean, and the ocean cannot be separated from the wave.

Continual cycles, constant change

When we learn to look deeply, to contemplate and to develop awareness, we come to see another key aspect of the universe, which is very much related to the idea that we are all interconnected; that we 'inter-are'. This is the cyclical, continually changing and self-renewing nature of life, of which we are of course part. Even as we meditate, we see how our mental states are always shifting and in motion; how one thought gives way to another; how one feeling or sensation will always transform into something else. We see the same principle at work in the natural world: the endless cycle of birth and death; the shifting of the seasons; the coming and going of the tides and the waxing and waning moon; the way in which nature continually reabsorbs the old and recycles it into the new.

Optical delusion

These deep realizations about the nature of life will bring about a radical shift in our perspective as human beings. As I have said, they are truths we all know instinctively; however, because of the way our society has developed and the way we consequently live our daily lives – especially in recent times – many of us have lost touch with these wisdoms and, in doing so, with our true nature. The consequences of forgetting, of losing sight of who we are and of our place in the larger scheme of things, have been catastrophic in many ways, leading us to decimate our planet, ignore the plight of our fellow men and women, and find ourselves as individuals overwhelmed by a tsunami of fear, anxiety and depression.

It was actually one of humanity's greatest scientists, Albert Einstein, who brilliantly summed up the devastating impact of our human tendency to lose touch with reality in this way:

'A human being is part of the whole called
by us "the universe", a part limited in
time and space. He experiences himself,
his thoughts and feelings, as something
separate from the rest – a kind of "optical
delusion" of consciousness. This delusion
is a kind of prison for us, restricting us
to our personal desires and affection of a
few persons nearest to us. Our task must
be to free ourselves from this prison by
widening our circle of understanding and
compassion to embrace all living creatures
and the whole of nature in its beauty.'

Resting in the heart of understanding

Through the practice of mindfulness, we can access the truth about life and our place in it, and keep it to the forefront of our awareness. This in turn enables us to break out of our self-imposed limits of believing that we are separate entities, with no deep sense of connection between us. When we realize that we are inextricably bound together, with each other and with the universe as a whole, we are released from the fear of death and can live in peace and contentment. We rest in the heart of understanding; we see things as they really are.

This awareness means that, instead of regarding others as a potential threat to everything that we have and that we are, we realize that we are as dependent on them as they are on us; that we are all facing the same struggle to be free from suffering; that we have so much more in common than we ever realized before. We find ourselves flooded with a deep sense of compassion, for others, for ourselves and for all living beings, in seeing that we are each just trying to navigate life as best we can in the circumstances in which we find ourselves. Feelings of greed, acquisitiveness and possessiveness, and antagonism towards the people we encounter in life, begin to fall away and are replaced by a profound sense of empathy – and indeed love – for our fellow human beings and indeed all forms of life on this planet.

Instead of fear, there is a profound sense of comfort in knowing that countless generations, before and after us, have been, and will go, through the same experiences as us; have felt the same feelings of fear and love and longing. Even in terms of death, there is a deep consolation and comfort in the knowledge that so many have gone before us – and will follow after us. People we have loved and known intimately, as well as people we never knew, but with whom we have so much in common.

No more rush to judgement

In realizing that everything is interconnected, our need to continually judge people and experiences falls by the wayside. Labels are dropped and intolerance dissipates.

As we settle further into this deep knowledge of reality, we see our opinions simply for what they are – useless defences of our unfounded fears and prejudices, of our own sense of a separate self. We come to see that there is no difference between me and you, between the homeless person and the rich man or woman, between the immigrant and the person who was born in *our* country, between those who see themselves as powerful and the disenfranchised. We all *inter-are*.

> I am here§ because you are here, and
> vice versa – literally and not literally.

As we see the deep connections between ourselves and our fellow human beings, and between all of us and life itself, our sense of loneliness disperses and we realize that we are part of something far greater; that we are no longer alone. As we continue with our everyday activities and with our journey in life, we carry with us a profound sense of belonging and the rightness of our being here.

The development of your awareness through the practice of mindfulness allows you to see the truth that you are made of 'non-you' things. You are made of your parents, and the entire human lineage that came before them. You are made of the same basic elements that are shared by every other living being and by non-living things alike. Elements that came into being billions of years ago and made gasses, metal, planets and stars, and that eventually led to you. You are made of rain and clouds, of the food you eat, and the earth it came from. You are made of the influences countless other people have had on you, and of the countless experiences you have had yourself.

> We all exist because the causes and conditions were present to bring us into existence, and we continue to exist because we all 'inter-are'.

These are the deep insights which come from directly experiencing life as it is, without passing through concepts and the constructs of thought. These are the rewards of meditation, of formal practice and living mindfully. The incredibly liberating and enriching impact of such wisdom on our lives is hard to sum up or express – again, you will only truly understand what I am talking about whenever you have deeply *known* these things for yourself. I feel however that these beautiful lines (which have only ever been attributed to an anonymous source) come close to capturing something of what I am trying to say:

> *'The moment you realize your bones are*
> *made of the same dust as the planets,*
> *your lungs are breathing the same air*
> *as the migrating butterflies, and your*
> *blood is pumping because of the love*
> *and care of thousands; [this] is when*
> *you realize you are not as broken as you*
> *think you are. You are full of the world.'*

Part IV

A NEW WAY OF BEING

Chapter 8

Fear

*'For there is nothing either good or
bad, but thinking makes it so.'*
WILLIAM SHAKESPEARE, *HAMLET*

We live in an age of anxiety as never before. Perhaps every generation has had this thought about the time in which they live, but I do think that there are real grounds for believing that our Western society today is more fearful than it has ever been. According to the World Health Organization (WHO), the prevalence of anxiety and depression (which often present together as emotional difficulties) in the global population has been increasing exponentially in recent years, and reaching what could be considered as epidemic proportions in many countries. Between 1990 and 2013, the number of people suffering from depression and/or anxiety increased by nearly 50 per cent – from 416 million to

615 million. Close to 10 per cent of the world's population is affected, while chronic, 'milder' mental disorders such as these account for 30 per cent of the global non-fatal disease burden. In areas where there are humanitarian emergencies and ongoing conflict, the WHO estimates that as many as one in five people are affected by depression and anxiety.[8]

For those of us lucky enough to live in countries where there are rarely widespread emergency situations, it seems, ironically, that the less we have to contend with in terms of real, immediate threats to our wellbeing, the more anxious we have become. Many of us see increasing evidence of this in our everyday lives.

Park incident

A year or so ago, I remember being in a fairly run-of-the-mill situation which brought this reality home to me in a very compelling way. It was a fine, sunny afternoon and I'd taken my two boys to our local park to play. It was just after school and the playground was packed with kids of various ages, all needing to let off steam.

Like most town play parks, ours has several sets of swings, a few climbing frames, a slide and so on, with large areas in between for children to run around. As usual, a number of parents, including me, had installed themselves on the park benches around the play area, so that we could keep an eye on our kids, and pass the time of day with each other as we waited.

Suddenly, there was a shrill, heart-wrenching cry – the kind every parent dreads. A girl, maybe three or four years old, had fallen from the top of the slide, hitting her head on the side of the steps on her way down and landing with a thud on the ground. We all saw her fall – and watched in horror as she did so. And we continued to watch, transfixed, as she lay there, crying in shock and pain.

After a few moments, during which no one moved, I jumped up and ran over to the child. 'Are you OK, love? Don't be frightened – just stay there – Mummy or Daddy will be here in a second!' As I scoured the playground, looking for an approaching parent, I suddenly realized that none of the other adults had budged – they were all just sitting there, stock-still, staring in dismay and disbelief. Many of the other children had run to their parents, and were clutching them and crying at the distressing sight of the injured toddler lying on the ground.

Even allowing for the shock of seeing the child falling, which kept us all frozen to the spot for the first few moments, I now found myself feeling baffled and a little annoyed that I was the only one to have run to her aid. Meanwhile, her mother arrived, puffing and panting, and crying out to her little girl. She told me, in an agonized voice, that she'd just been briefly to another part of the park, to put some leftovers from the kids' snacks in the bin, and had asked one of her older children to keep an eye on his sister during the time she was away. He'd run to get her as soon as he saw the child falling.

Fortunately, as it turned out, the little girl wasn't badly hurt. Once her mother arrived, she calmed down quickly and didn't seem in any obvious pain. The mother decided to take her to the local hospital casualty department to be checked out, and called me later, to let me know that everything was fine – no lasting damage done, thankfully. She'd insisted on taking my number, as she was so grateful I'd run over to her daughter to try to help during the time she was absent herself.

'If you hadn't done that, she would have just been left lying there all by herself, with nobody to comfort her,' she said, as she left the park. In this, without actually saying it out loud, she was acknowledging that no one else had budged from their benches to help a small child in distress.

As we drove home afterwards – my boys were subdued, still a little shaken from the incident – I kept thinking back to what had happened, and the fact that all the other adults had stayed where they were, apparently almost more terrified of the situation than the child who'd fallen.

Later that evening, I mentioned what had happened to some friends I was meeting at the pub for a quick drink. Everyone said the same thing: 'Sure, you know that's what it's like these days. In a situation like that, especially when a very young child is involved, people are afraid to do anything. Just say the kid was badly injured, and they ran over to help and moved her in the wrong way? If she'd hurt her neck or back, they might be responsible for paralysing her, or making the damage far worse in some other way.'

I agreed that these fears seemed reasonable enough to me – you'd have to be very careful not to move someone, in the case of a possible back injury. But, I asked, why should that stop you from running over to check on a child who'd fallen?

Again, the others all came with the similar theories on that point. 'Well, if you went near her and she was badly injured, even if you didn't move her, there's a chance her parents could put in a huge claim against you, and you might be dragged through the courts and find yourself involved in a legal process liable to last months.'

Someone else suggested that it would probably all be reported in the local papers, and from then on, everyone would think of you as the person who'd ruined a child's life. Or even that, by going over to help and comfort an injured child, you could lay yourself open to suspicion about your motives for doing so – maybe you'd be seen as taking an unhealthy interest in the child... And so on, and so forth.

After this conversation, I found myself thinking once again – it certainly wasn't the first time in recent years – about the ridiculous levels of anxiety we've created in our society. We're so afraid of everything, so paranoid about being held to account, legally and financially, for the smallest, most apparently harmless thing, so busy trying to second-guess the consequences of the most seemingly innocent and loving actions on our part, that we hold ourselves back from doing the most natural, and human, and compassionate thing in the world – such as running to help a small child in distress. We're all too aware that everywhere, there are people actively seeking to find offence in anything we might say (unintentionally and without the least thought of disrespecting someone or hurting their feelings), who won't hesitate to shame us on social media; we might even end up being targeted by trolls, or becoming the subject of some kind of Facebook campaign, and so on.

What a society we have created – and
how much we need to change, and liberate
ourselves from this stifling culture of anxiety
and self-protection. We so badly need to be
able to act more spontaneously – in kind,
compassionate and humane ways – without
expecting the sky to fall down upon us!

If we add these very modern fears to all the other worries many of us have – about losing our job, becoming ill, losing our spouse, about the possibility of something happening to our children, being alone, losing our reputation, our standard of living, or even our home – and of course, the big one: the fear of death itself – we can see just how much fear and anxiety dominate the lives of so many of us. It's a wonder anybody can find one moment of peace and contentment in the day. And of course, as we know, many of us can't.

One of the most heartbreaking examples in my own recent experience, of the extent to which fear has gripped our society, cropped up not so long ago when I was delivering a workshop in Belfast. I'd been talking about anxiety and psychological fear, and how unhelpful and limiting they so often are, and in the Q&A session afterwards, a lady in the audience raised her hand to say that in her experience, this type of fear was a good thing. When I asked her why, she recounted the following story…

Love not fear

Eight years ago, my son emigrated to Australia. It broke my heart to see him go, but I knew it was what he wanted to do and that he wasn't happy here in Ireland. Everything went well in the beginning, and he got a job and a place to live and made some good friends. After a while, he started seeing a lovely girl and before long, they moved in together.

But three years ago, things started to go downhill for my son, and he became depressed. His phone calls home became less frequent and sometimes he wouldn't return my calls. I was so worried, I couldn't sleep… He was so far away, and I felt useless and unable to help. Then one day last year, we got a call from my son's girlfriend in the middle of the night. She was very upset, saying she didn't know what to do – she told me that my son was talking about killing himself.

I've never been more afraid in my life and the next day I got on a plane to Australia. I needed to be with him, to tell him how loved he was, that he wasn't alone, and that I and his Dad and all his family were here to support him. I wanted to show him that distance and time wouldn't stop us from being there for him when he needed us…

So, you see, this is why I think fear is a good thing. If I hadn't been so afraid of my son killing himself, I wouldn't have gone to Australia to spend time with him, and he wouldn't be alive and well today. That's why I believe this kind of fear can help us.

I was very troubled to hear this story – not only due to the story itself, but because this incredible, caring mother really believed that fear had caused her to travel halfway around the world to be with her son. Fear had nothing to do with it – it was this lady's fierce *love* for her son that was the driving force behind her actions. Love took her to Australia. The impulse to, above all, care for her son was the reason she needed so badly to be with him, to tell him how much he was loved and valued, and to explain to him that nothing would keep her from being there for him. Fear never generates kindness, compassion, caring or courage – these things are the product of love, and love alone. When I said this to this lady, she broke down and cried. I think she was finally allowing herself to accept what an incredibly loving mother and person she was, and to acknowledge that her son was alive today because of her love and not her fear.

I described this story earlier as a heartbreaking example of how fear is taking over our society, because it is clear that this mother had defaulted to thinking that she must have acted out of fear, and wasn't even able to recognize her huge, selfless love for her son.

Types of fear

It's important here to make the distinction between the different types of fear. As I see things, there are two main kinds of fear which are relevant here – and for clarity's sake, I will refer to these, respectively, as physical fear and psychological fear.

Physical fear generally arises as a direct response to a specific danger, something which is an immediate threat to our physical wellbeing. We see a car approaching a little too fast as we are crossing the road, and so we jump out of the way to avoid getting physically hurt or worse. When our ancient ancestors saw danger in the offing in the form of a charging lion or bear, they did everything they could to remove themselves from the situation, as an instinctive fight-or-flight response kicked in – the same physiological response that we experience and keeps us safe from physical danger. In these instances, fear serves a very useful purpose and is clearly a good thing in that context.

The second main type of fear is something very different, however. It tends to be a more generalized feeling, which can't be pinned down to anything specific in the immediate present in terms of a physical threat. This kind of psychological fear, or anxiety, is always born of thought – from either ruminating on something that has happened in the past and fearing it may somehow catch up with us now, or from projecting present anxieties into the future, and worrying about things which haven't happened yet (and most often never will). This kind of fear or anxiety is never based in the present, but always concerns itself with something that has already happened, or may yet happen.

Perhaps you were seriously ill two years ago, and even though you are back to full health now, and this has been confirmed by your doctor, thoughts begin to tell you otherwise: *You'd better be careful – whatever you do, you don't want to get sick again!* In time this type of thinking creates the physical manifestations of fear. However, although the anxiety might feel very real in this sense, even physically, it is not actually based on fact – since the present reality is that you are fit as a fiddle! And yet we can see how thought has created and reinforced the fear of becoming ill so powerfully that it feels very real to us.

Incidentally, this kind of psychological fear is something that cancer survivors often find that they struggle greatly with. They've been given the all-clear, and feel so lucky to be alive and well – but every time they have a sore throat or a minor fever or are feeling very tired, thought begins to work on them, and quickly creates the fear that the cancer may be back. In fact, some cancer survivors go on to suffer from PTSD (post-traumatic stress disorder), as a result.[9] Such anxiety is of course in many ways, perfectly understandable in these specific circumstances. However, it may well have no basis in reality whatsoever in instances where the person really does just have a cold or sore throat, as the symptoms of a common cold.

A self-fulfilling prophesy

However, there are very many occasions when, rationally speaking, the fears we project into the future are utterly unfounded and unjustified – and completely obstructive to our wellbeing in the present. Perhaps, for example, your ex-partner cheated on you a number of times – does this automatically mean that the same thing will happen in any future relationships you have? Your father died when you were very young – does this imply that everyone you get close to in adult life will end up leaving or abandoning you in one way or another? Maybe you were nervous and unprepared for an important interview, and ended up making a mess of it and losing out on the job – but does this mean that, going forwards, you'll automatically do the same thing every time you are interviewed for a job you really want? And there are many other mundane situations where we can let anxiety take over, without even being able to pinpoint its source. For instance, some parents experience a great deal of anxiety about letting their children out to play outdoors. If you ask them what exactly they are afraid of, their answers are almost always very vague and not based on any actual event or past experience.

In all of these cases, there is nothing in the immediate present that justifies the anxiety someone is experiencing. And the plain fact is that, in the absence of immediate, discernible danger to our physical wellbeing, we very seldom have anything to worry about in the present moment. When you are confronted with something which threatens you physically and immediately, there is no fear, just action. The insidious thing about the baseless anxieties created by thought is that, ultimately, they can have the effect of a self-fulfilling prophesy – i.e. influence our responses, our decisions and our general mind-set that they end up creating the very situations which we most feared.

We've all seen this at work... Normally a confident public speaker, you have one episode of stage fright that affects you so badly, you begin to anticipate that the same thing will happen again each time you have to give a presentation – you expect the worst, and so you create the conditions for the worst to happen. A top golfer loses his nerve during a crucial championship game, and afterwards becomes engulfed in the anxiety that the same thing will keep happening each time he's in the spotlight. And sadly, this is exactly what happens, precisely because he spent so much time ruminating on past failure.

Not only can fear limit our potential and prevent us from achieving what we want to, in terms of our talents and abilities in our professional or personal ventures, but it can also hold us back in a much more general way – preventing us from achieving our full potential as emotional, loving human beings interacting with those around us and the people we love. The earlier story about not helping a small child in distress is an example of this, and there are so many others... In our age of paranoia and extreme political correctness, we are afraid of being generous and spontaneous in our encounters with others. We hold back from gestures of kindness towards strangers – helping an elderly person pick up the shopping items they've dropped; asking a young girl we see crying and in distress as we walk along the street if she is OK and needs any help; smiling and saying hello to someone whose eye catches ours in the street; paying someone a compliment or exchanging a few words to pass the time of day. We hold back too with those we know well – not freely giving praise or compliments, or expressing feelings of warmth and connection.

> As fear gains ground and becomes more widespread in the general population, our world becomes a colder, poorer and less generous place.

How mindfulness helps

Mindfulness can help us immensely in dealing with, and diminishing, these 'thought-made' fears. In the most direct, immediate way, as we become more aware of our mental processes and feelings, mindfulness allows us to create a space between our thoughts and emotions and how we respond to them. This in turn gives us the opportunity to challenge the rationale and the reality of our anxieties.

In this context, where you are feeling overwhelmed by worry and negative speculation about the past or future, a good question to always ask yourself is, 'What's wrong *right now*?'

So often, the answer is that there is absolutely nothing to be afraid of in the present moment. In this way, mindfulness brings us back time and again to the reality that so many of our anxieties are groundless, and helps to free us from the limiting prison of fear.

Fear often springs from a disconnection from the truth – the truth about life, the truth of our circumstances and, above all, the truth of who we really are. Notably, when we lose a sense of ourselves, we find that our fears grow, as they feed off each other and multiply. However by living mindfully through formal mindfulness practice and consciously bringing its insights into our everyday lives, we can stay connected to our essential selves, and keep in touch with who we are; this realization in turn allows us to be less fearful.

How awareness helps

As we reach higher levels of awareness, the insights about life that we gain, and which become part of our natural way of being, will continue to work to diminish the levels of fear in our lives. So much of our fear is bound up with the possibility of losing what we have, but when we live with the reality of impermanence, we become increasingly aware of the pointlessness of fearing loss before it actually happens.

If everything is impermanent, including everything we have, the people we are closest to and we ourselves as beings, we know and must accept that loss is inevitable; that it is part of life. With this realization and profound level of acceptance, so many of our fears somehow dissipate. When trying to get to grips with anxiety and reduce its hold on us, meditating on the truth of impermanence can really help – try the Meditation on Impermanence at the end of Chapter 6.

Testimonials from people who have attended my workshops, and who have introduced mindful practice into their daily lives, seem to bear out this sense of a general reduction of fear and anxiety levels. Small changes can be just as significant as more dramatic ones in this context. For example, Orla Carney, a member of our regular events team, recounts that for many years, before practising mindfulness, she was terrified of spiders – almost to the point of phobia. 'I used to scream and run away in a panic whenever I caught sight of a spider in one of our rooms at home – even very small spiders would have that effect on me.' Since practising mindfulness on a regular basis, however, Orla has noticed a big change: 'I'm not quite sure of how or why, but now, when I see a spider, I feel completely calm and don't even flinch. I even find myself feeling sorry for it, and try to make sure that it gets out of the house without being harmed.'

My wife, Faye, has had the same experience in relation to public speaking. 'I've always dreaded the idea of having to give a speech, or address any group of more than about 10 people. If I did find myself in such a situation, I'd get incredibly nervous, feel physically sick and, while speaking, would have to battle with all the symptoms of stage fright – dry mouth, trembling hands, shaky voice and knocking knees. But since I started doing formal daily mindfulness practice, I've noticed how much calmer and more composed I feel when speaking in front of a big group. While I wouldn't say I actually enjoy it or seek out opportunities to do it, I no longer feel panicky, and I can get through it without any of the old drama.'

As I have been saying throughout this book, my own experience has been that awareness has transformed my responses to life in more general, profound ways too. Nowhere has this been truer than when it comes to fear and the kinds of reactions it engenders. I began this chapter by telling you about the incident I witnessed not so long ago, when a small child fell from a slide in the park and, other than me, no one ran to help her or check that she was OK. I'm in no way trying to portray myself as some kind of saint or hero by mentioning that I went over straight away to comfort this injured little girl – the truth is, if I'd found myself in the same situation 10–12 years ago, I would have reacted as everyone else did that day, and been afraid to go near her. Before taking up my practice and working on my awareness, my own default mode was, in tricky social situations like these, to avoid getting involved at all costs. I guess my reluctance to get involved came from the same place as many other people's – a fear of finding myself out of my depth, in unpredictable circumstances where I couldn't necessarily foresee or control the outcome. Thankfully, I have been able to move beyond this kind of thinking now, and am no longer afraid to spontaneously step in and do or say what the situation calls for – but it took a long time for me to get to this place.

I'll give you another quick example of how my perspective has changed in this way.

Lunchtime dilemmas

The other day, when I was coming out of Marks & Spencer in Dublin with my two sons – we'd just been buying some sandwiches for lunch – the boys stopped to talk to a homeless guy who was sitting in the large doorway of the shop.

After a few moments we moved on, but very quickly, Tiernan and Odhrán asked me to slow down, saying that they wanted to give some of our sandwiches to the homeless man. And so we made our way back to the shop to do this. Although you'd think I would always be pleased that my sons would want to do something generous like this, I know for a fact that in the past, I would have just hurried them on, telling them we simply didn't have time to go back to see this guy and give him the sandwiches. I know that, unless we were indeed in a great hurry (which we weren't that day), my impulse would have been to shy away from the unscripted involvement in this situation, because it wasn't one I knew I would have control over – just say the homeless guy didn't appreciate the gesture, and began shouting at us, threatening us, or worse? And what about other people around us – what might they think, or do, or say? And so on.

For me today, however, these kinds of fears, which only act to limit our potentially positive, loving instincts and actions, are very much a thing of the past – and I'm free to respond spontaneously and with generosity and kindness in these types of situations and many more besides.

Less fear, more inclusiveness

Another key insight, which we explored in Chapter 7, is that of the interconnectedness of all things in this world, and indeed in this life. Once we live with an ever-present sense of this truth, we find that many of our fears begin to fall away, almost of their own accord. As we see more clearly how all people and all things are related to and, ultimately dependent on each other for their existence, we realize too that we have less to fear from others than we might have imagined; that we are not the separate, entirely self-contained entities we thought we were. The ego diminishes, and with this, we find that we have less to lose and less to defend against when it comes to other people – we realize that what we have in common with others is so much more real and more powerful than the things we previously believed separated us.

We realize that we need others, and that they need us, in very fundamental ways. We looked at this in depth in the last chapter. For example, in order to come into existence in the first place, we need others – our parents; and to continue to exist in the most concrete sense, we need others too: to be able to eat, drink, have a roof over our heads, and have many of our other basic needs met. We realize that we need the fabric and structures of our human society in order to simply lead our lives on a day-to-day basis. And beyond this, we become more fully aware of the extent to which we are all bound together by our common experience and our shared circumstances: being born into this world, and trying to make our way through life as best we can, all of us facing the reality of impermanence and personal suffering.

Recognizing self-limiting values

These deep insights – about the reality of impermanence and the extent to which we are all inextricably connected, with each other and with life itself – inevitably lead us to challenge many of the values and beliefs that society has imposed on us since we were small children, and which lie at the heart of many of our most limiting and unhelpful fears.

We've been told, for example, that competition is the only way. As soon as we start school, at the age of four or five, we learn that life is all about being better than everyone else, or at least being better than the child next to us if nothing else – at arithmetic, at writing, at drawing, and so on. And from the beginning, we are constantly pushed to be better than ourselves – better than our last performance or exam result, better than we were yesterday, last week, or last year. It's not about helping other people, and so often not about working together to achieve something as a team – it's about fulfilling your own potential, focusing on your individual achievements, *being better*, and getting more, than your peers.

Of course, there is nothing wrong with making the most of your own talents, and trying to improve yourself – especially if your skills and abilities will be put to use helping other people and improving life for everyone. In this sense, someone who is a gifted artist has as much of a contribution to make as an accomplished scientist. But because so much of the emphasis from our earliest years is on trying to outdo each other, we are given the message loud and clear that being competitive is key to what we do in life.

The damaging, toxic effect of living competitively becomes clear when we realize how much fear it generates in our lives. Whether we are aware of it or not – and it can be quite a shock when we do realize it – constantly comparing ourselves to others is at the heart of so much of the anxiety we feel. We are afraid of not being as good as the guy next door; we are afraid of our colleagues at work, in case they try to undermine us and get the recognition we feel should be ours; we are afraid of foreigners coming into our community, in case they take what we regard as ours... Most ridiculously, we are afraid of ourselves – afraid of not being as good as we were in the past; afraid of not measuring up in a projected future to what we are in the present. No wonder we're all so anxious!

Living mindfully, and working to develop our awareness, allows us to cut through all of this false fear, and enables us to see the toxic and limiting nature of some of the key values we've been told are important.

Once we can do this, we can choose for ourselves a way of living which is free of fear, and greed and always grasping for more.

Tonglen Meditation – for Fear

This meditation exercise for relieving fear draws on a few different techniques, including *tonglen*, which is normally used as a loving-kindness practice (tonglen is a Tibetan word for 'sending and taking' or 'giving and receiving'). However, a number of people I have suggested use this exercise have found it very useful in dispersing fearful feelings.

Psychological fear comes in many guises – anxiety, worry, guilt, catastrophizing – the list goes on... whenever these feelings threaten to take over, and you have the opportunity, try the following **Tonglen Meditation**.

Sit quietly in a place where you won't be disturbed. Close your eyes and focus your awareness on your breath.

Ask yourself the question: 'What's wrong right now; right in this moment?' Not what is your mind saying is wrong, but *what is actually happening right now* that you need to be afraid of? Examine your situation and get to a place where you can recognize and accept the fact that, right now in this moment, there is nothing to fear.

Acknowledge that, although there is nothing to fear or worry or be anxious about right now, fear or worry or anxiety are still present. Try to sense the place in your body that is experiencing the fear most – do you have a knot in your stomach, a tight chest, tense shoulders?

Scanning the body slowly, now identify exactly where the feeling is most intense. Once you have done this, start to relax the parts of the body that are not affected. In particular, try to relax all the areas *around* where you are experiencing the feeling of fear in your body. For example, if your chest is tight, relax your shoulders and your neck. If you have a burn of anxiety in your stomach, relax the chest and arms, and so on.

Now, say internally these words to your fear/anxiety/worry: 'I know you are there and that you are part of me, yet I also know that there is nothing wrong in this moment. But I have made room for you and I will look after you for as long as you are around.'

At this point, imagine that your energy of mindful awareness is going directly to the part of your body that is experiencing the feeling most intensely, and that this energy is holding the fear or anxiety in the way a mother would hold a child. Imagine your energy of awareness wrapping the energy of fear or worry in a blanket of loving-kindness. Stay with this until the fearful feeling dissipates.

Once you feel more at ease, call to mind the millions of people in this world suffering in the same way as you – those who suffer from fear, anxiety, worry and the need to blame. Bring your attention and awareness to your breath. Imagine breathing in the pain of all these people. You can picture their suffering as a kind of smoky air. As you breathe their suffering in, direct it to the same place in your body where you felt your own fear or anxiety the most.

Next bring the same energy of loving-kindness to the suffering of others as you did to your own suffering. As you breathe out, imagine your energy of awareness and loving-kindness removing the suffering. You can picture this out-breath as bright, clear light and direct it to all those who are suffering stress, anxiety, worry or any of the other forms of fear.

Chapter 9

'Difficult' Emotions:
How Awareness Dilutes
Their Power

*'There are people moving around us who are
consumed by their past, terrified of their future,
and stuck in their anger and jealousy. They are
not alive; they are just walking corpses.'*

THICH NHAT HANH

At the beginning of this book, I made the important point that the intense, strongly negative emotions that all of us feel at times – and which are referred to euphemistically as 'difficult' or 'challenging' feelings – are the stuff of the innate, personal suffering each of us goes through in life. The suffering each individual undergoes will of course be unique and distinctive to that person, depending on such factors as their circumstances, history, perspective and bank of past experiences, and so on. And even our unique biochemical makeup will play its part here. However, the main types of emotions – love, hate, anger, fear, jealousy, possessiveness and so on – are universally felt by us all, and in this sense, as in many others, there is a huge territory of common ground between all of us.

In previous chapters, we have seen the various ways in which practising mindfulness and building awareness can help us to deal with and minimize our everyday personal suffering. In this chapter, I'd like to look in more detail at some practical strategies that can help us manage strong, negative emotions, as well as further exploring how deeper levels of awareness will lend us a different, transformative perspective on personal suffering.

In this book so far, we have already considered some of the intense, primary emotions which cause us most suffering. In Chapter 2, with the story of the husband and the loaf of bread, we saw Mary's anger at Joe's absentmindedness, and the all-too-familiar scenario of a trivial domestic incident sparking a surprisingly disproportionate response. We then looked at the ways in which practising mindfulness and developing awareness would have helped Mary to short-circuit her anger, enabling her to identify it earlier, better understand it and, as a result, deal with the situation in a more measured way – resulting in less unnecessary suffering for herself and those around her.

In Chapter 6, we saw the fear and insecurity experienced by John in the early stages of his relationship with Denise, and how the simple fact that one evening she didn't answer the phone unleashed a torrent of self-doubt and mental torment for him. I suggested that if John had had greater awareness and the deep knowledge of life's impermanence which awareness brings, he would have been able to resist the urge to cling more tightly to his new love interest the minute he felt that she might be slipping from his grasp. Knowing the transient nature of his relationship with Denise, and indeed of life itself, he would have realized the futility of his fears of loss and his attempts to hold on; he would have been able to focus instead on appreciating Denise, and their connection, all the more intensely in the present.

In the same chapter, very much related to this, we also looked at the powerful emotion of the grief of bereavement. I talked about my own grief in relation to losing my mother, Rosie, and prior to this my two brothers, Dan and Denny. I described – or at least, did my best to convey – how my work in developing awareness, which I began after the deaths of my brothers, changed the way I experienced the later loss of my mother.

We saw that a deep acceptance of the inevitability of loss, and of the impermanence of all things in this life, didn't make my mourning any less intense, but did mean that my feelings of grief were somehow purer and more real. The pain I felt was more about the loss of the person themselves than about my self-focused feelings that their death was something that had been *done* to me.

On a less serious note, in Chapter 2, we looked at the previously puzzling sense of embarrassment and shame I used to feel when hanging out our family laundry in the back garden. Drilling down to what really lay behind these feelings, I was able to identify some distorted and slightly ridiculous ideas about the world and my place in it, which I never even guessed I'd been carrying around with me for so long. The same kind of distorted thinking as that which would have previously stirred feelings of annoyance in me at the sight of a pair of socks lying on our living room floor – because of my long-held belief that such casual actions by others were an indication that they didn't rate me as a person.

In all of these instances, we saw how many of the *big* truths about life, which awareness allows us to grasp with great clarity – such as the reality of impermanence, the fact that we are all intimately connected with each other and with everything in the universe and the fact that we normally live our lives through layers of opinions, prejudices and fears – work to radically change our overall way of seeing things, and help us to better navigate our everyday suffering.

Now, let's look at some more focused, practical strategies for handling strong and potentially overwhelming emotions. These strategies are in many ways a natural progression from the practice of mindfulness, and can as such be integrated into our formal practice and mindful daily living. With continued practise, they work to lessen our suffering, and allow us to live with greater ease.

RAIN

In outlining the following practical steps for dealing with the suffering caused by difficult feelings or emotions, I am drawing on an established mindfulness practice known as 'RAIN', which was originally devised by Michele McDonald, a highly respected Buddhist teacher and author who has been teaching Insight Meditation for over 25 years from her base in Hawaii (and indeed all over the world).

RAIN is an acronym for the four stages proposed in this practice, which incorporates the core teachings of mindfulness, and its letters stand for:

Recognize, Accept, Investigate, and Non-identification.

Approaching painful emotions in this manner can help us gain deeper self-knowledge and wisdom, and transform the suffering of intense negative emotions into more workable and indeed actively enlightening experiences. Practising RAIN can also help us avoid falling into default, unhelpful responses – such as obsessive rumination or impulsively acting out.

The basic principle behind **RAIN** is that when difficult emotions arise, we should practice working with them by **recognizing**, **accepting**, **investigating** and **not identifying** with whatever is present. In theory, RAIN can be brought to any situation you may find emotionally challenging. This can include everyday low-level annoyances – such as irritation at the constant, tinny sound of elevator music, which is always playing when you're shopping at your local supermarket, or the noise of your fellow train passenger on your daily commute compulsively clicking his pen as you're trying to read, or the noise the couple behind you in the cinema are making as they chomp their way through a vat of popcorn. The list is endless!

You can also apply RAIN to more challenging emotions, such as anger at your partner, the disappointment at losing out on a much-wanted job or promotion, or persistent feelings of loneliness or grief, or even the emotional fallout of some kind of serious trauma.

However, particularly if you are new to mindfulness and formal meditation practice, I would counsel caution, especially initially, when using the RAIN approach since dealing with difficult emotional experiences in this way can be very powerful and you may quickly begin to feel overwhelmed. For this reason, I recommend that to start off with, you practise using the approach for relatively small stuff – such as the kinds of minor annoyances I've mentioned above. Step three – Investigation – can prove particularly challenging, especially in relation to very traumatic experiences and so, again, I'd advise getting some practice with the other steps in the process first.

It can also be very helpful to practise RAIN in meditation initially, in relation to a low-key past experience, before moving on to drawing on it in your everyday processing of emotions as they arise in the present. We'll look more closely at how to make RAIN part of your meditation practice towards the end of this chapter. And finally, if at any time you begin to feel overwhelmed by the process of investigating your feelings in a given situation, or when re-creating them imaginatively after the event, as you can do in a meditation, it is also best to gently stop and leave things for the time being.

RAIN

~

Step 1: Recognize

The first step to working with a difficult emotion is to recognize when it is present. As we saw in Chapter 2, when Mary exploded with rage because her husband Joe forgot to get the bread she'd asked for, developing the ability to recognize our feelings as early as possible can buy us crucial time, by allowing us to see what is happening before we feel swamped by intense emotion and end up lashing out at other people.

Recognizing your emotions as they arise involves pausing and asking yourself, 'What am I experiencing right now in this situation – in my body, in my thinking and in my emotions?' What physical sensations are you most aware of? A burning sensation in your stomach, or the feeling of tension rising in your chest, or the tightening of the muscles in your neck and shoulders – or all of these together – likely mean that you're feeling anger. A sinking feeling in your stomach, the sensation of a lump in your throat, or the pricking of tears in your eyes most probably indicate that you are feeling upset and hurt by what someone has said or done... And so on. Of course, we all experience the physical effects of different emotions in different ways – and so, it is up to each of us to become familiar with our own reactions and responses, and so we can start to recognize what certain physical sensations indicate about how we are feeling and thinking.

Next, try to connect with what you are thinking – is your mind churning with thoughts? Are those thoughts very fast-moving and increasingly agitated; do they really reflect what is happening right now, or are they out of all proportion to the current situation you find yourself in?

Recognizing prevents denial or avoidance because you are deliberately bringing what is unpleasant, and perhaps unwholesome, into the forefront of your awareness, so that it can be seen for what it is, and dealt with. In this process, it can be helpful to try to internally sum up in words what exactly the feeling or thought is – for example, 'I am feeling stressed,' or 'I am feeling overwhelmed.' This recognition of what you are feeling has the effect of opening up some inner space. This is turn allows you room to manoeuvre and brings you more fully into contact with yourself and with what is happening in the present.

We know from neuroscience and the results of brain imaging studies that consciously connecting with and labelling our emotions has the effect of reducing activity in the emotionally reactive regions of the brain. This makes it less likely that we will act out rashly, and in ways we might regret, to what is happening in that moment.

Step 2: Accept

The next step is to practise acceptance of whatever feelings or thoughts you are having in an emotionally fraught situation or encounter. Acceptance in this context means simply acknowledging what is present in this moment and allowing what is already here to just be here. It is important to note that, just because you accept or acknowledge that something is present, this doesn't imply that you are agreeing with or supporting it. You are simply recognizing what is present right now. So, you could just say to yourself, 'Anger is here,' or 'Sadness is here.'

During this stage of the process, try also to be aware of any thoughts or emotions that may arise as you acknowledge what you are experiencing. You may feel aversion or even self-loathing, for example, when you have to recognize the fact that you are vulnerable enough to have become upset by something someone has said – since this may not fit into your idea of yourself as a strong, self-confident person who is not bothered by what other people think. Notice too any subtle or unconscious forms of resisting your emotions, such as trying to *accept* them so that they will go away – which really entails trying to push away and deny what is happening now.

See if you can truly allow what is here to simply be here, and try to let the emotion run its natural course and leave in its own time. When practising acceptance in this way, you may find it helpful to say such words or phrases to yourself as 'Yes', or 'Allow'.

In this context – the practice of recognizing and accepting what we are feeling at any given moment – a good analogy I draw on in my workshops, and which people tell me they find very useful, is that of a mother and a child. Whenever you experience a distressing emotion – such as anger, upset, fear – which will not abate and keeps coming back to you, think of yourself as the mother, and of the emotion or thought as your child. When a crying baby demands attention, a caring parent will want to comfort it, but also, importantly, to take control and make sure their child's needs are properly addressed. In many ways, your strong, extreme emotions are like an upset child – they are out of control, helpless and powerless, and in need of reassurance. It is up to you, like a good parent, to look after and soothe your emotions, and try to address what they are telling you by taking any action needed – but in a calm, considered and effective way.

So, the next time you feel very angry or upset about something someone has said or done, think of your anger or upset as that small child, and say something to yourself like, 'Anger, I know you're here and are trying to take over this situation – even though you won't be able to do the right thing about it. You can hang around for as long as you want to – that's OK with me; I'm not ordering you to leave. But I'm going to deal with this situation – you don't have to. Stay for as long as you need to, but I'll handle things from here.'

It's actually amazing what effect this approach can have when you're feeling very intense emotions. You'll probably find that once the emotion has your permission to stay for as long as it wants to, it will quickly lose interest, so to speak and, realizing that there's no more attention to be had and no lashing out to be done, will often just dissipate of its own accord. Try this for yourself the next time you're feeling very stressed or annoyed, and see what happens.

Step 3: Investigate

After working with recognizing and accepting what is present for you, you can now begin to investigate your internal experience. It is crucial to bring an attitude of kindness, curiosity and compassion to your investigation. Again, while doing this internal audit of your feelings, think of yourself as a parent – caring and kind, but also strong and capable of taking control when necessary.

As with Step 1 (recognition), begin by focusing on the physical sensations you are feeling. Notice any sensations present in your body at that moment – including where in the body you are feeling them. Perhaps you're aware of your heart apparently beating more loudly than normally, or that your heart rate has quickened; you may even feel the pounding of your heartbeat in your head, or hear it in your ears. You might feel an uncomfortable heat rising in your neck and flushing your face, a tingling feeling in your fingers or a wave of nervous energy washing through your stomach and prickling in your chest.

Now note the changing nature of these sensations – are they growing more, or less, intense; are they coming and going in waves; or are they steady and constant? As you focus on this, try to register anything else which occurs at a physical level.

Next, ask yourself again, 'What emotions am I experiencing right now?' This time, try to focus more intensely. Note the basic tone of your overall emotional state – is it negative, neutral or positive? Try to pinpoint more precisely what emotions are present: are you feeling fear, anger, annoyance, grief, shame, upset, hurt?

Now ask yourself, 'What does this feeling want from me right now? What is it trying to tell me?' In conducting this investigation, you are connecting more deeply with your present self – but you are also slowing things down internally, and creating some space which will enable you to choose what you might want or need to do next – rather than just being blindly carried away by your extreme emotions.

Finally, shift your attention to your thoughts. Note what thoughts are passing through your mind right now; look at the tenor of your thinking – negative, neutral, or positive? Are your thoughts speeding up, or slowing down, in this moment?

Now you can perhaps ask yourself, 'What stories am I believing right now?' Do you believe that you are failing in some way? That someone will reject you? That you will not be able to handle whatever is around the corner? That you really are flawed and that because of this, no one will ever really accept you? That you will never be happy?

Gently examine these thoughts as far as you can – but if, however, this becomes too much, simply drop this part of your investigation, and shift your focus back to your bodily sensations, or your overall emotional mood. Or move on to the next stage below – non-identification. As I said earlier, it's important to stop at any point – particularly during this investigation phase – if you begin to feel overwhelmed.

Step 4: Non-identification

Non-identification means not believing that your emotions *belong* to you, or labelling them as 'me' or 'mine'. It involves not taking emotions personally, and understanding that, whatever emotions you are feeling in any particular moment, they are not you, the entirety of who you are, even in that moment.

It can be very helpful to label the emotion you are experiencing as something that is present in this moment but not permanent – and also to pay closer attention to the way you refer to emotions generally. So, instead of saying, 'I am angry,' you could reframe things more accurately by saying, 'I am experiencing anger right now,' or even 'Anger is present right now.' As we have discussed previously, the thoughts we have and the way we frame things to ourselves internally is crucially important because this can have so much impact on how we feel.

Since identifying with how we are feeling is almost in-built in our English language – 'I am sad,' 'I am happy,' 'I am doubtful,' 'I am fearful' and so on – it can be even more difficult to break this habit of thinking that we become whatever emotion has taken hold of us in any given moment. But it's really worthwhile to make the conscious effort to reframe the situation more accurately, even as regards the language we use.

Interestingly, not all other languages operate in the way that English does in this context. In French, for example, it is *J'ai peur* (literally 'I have fear' = I am afraid) or *J'ai honte* ('I have shame' = I am ashamed) or even, *J'ai faim* ('I have hunger' = I am hungry). I'm not an expert in foreign languages – far from it, in fact – but even thinking back to my basic school French, this difference when talking about emotions and physical sensations always strikes me.

In any case, the fact remains that the thoughts and emotions you experience are not who you are. As I mentioned at the beginning of this chapter, your feelings are certainly not unique to you, but are experienced and suffered by all humans. And here again, it is the *big* realizations we have talked about in earlier chapters that can help us to gain a larger, more realistic perspective. The truth that life – and everything in it, including our emotions – is impermanent and ever-changing means that we know our emotional suffering will pass on to, or simply shift into, the next thing.

The reality that there is so much common ground between ourselves and all living beings, helps to increase our compassion for others, and, especially important in this present context, for ourselves – making it easier to be that caring parent when it comes to managing the feelings which make us suffer so much.

—

Using RAIN in formal meditation

As I said earlier, a very helpful way of familiarising yourself with the practice of RAIN, as a way of managing your emotions and achieving deeper self-knowledge, is to start by making it part of your formal meditation sessions. This is a gentler way of breaking yourself in to this practice, without having to deal with the stress of an immediate, actual situation, and the physical effects of intense, extreme emotions while you go through the steps.

Practising RAIN while meditating will make it much easier to apply the steps to situations as they happen in your life, when you are ready to do so. It will also enable you to achieve deeper insights during the course of your meditation practice about the situation or feelings you have chosen to focus on – which, in turn, you can feed into your growing overall awareness.

To begin, prepare yourself as you usually would just prior to formal meditation. Sit quietly, close your eyes, and focus on your breath for a few moments.

Now bring to mind a current situation in your life which is making you feel *stuck* and to which you find yourself reacting with emotions such as anger or fear, shame or hopelessness, frustration or powerlessness. This situation may be something like an ongoing or recent conflict with your partner, a failure at work, a physical ailment or a conversation you now regret.

As you sit in meditation, take some moments to enter into the experience – visualize the scene or situation and the person or people involved; recall the words spoken and the general tone of the encounter, gently bringing to your mind the most distressing moments and the physical and emotional reactions you had during these. Really try to put yourself back into the situation.

Now apply the four steps of RAIN, as set out above:

Recognize whatever thoughts, feelings and emotions are present as you bring the event to mind.

Accept that they are there, without judgement.

Investigate what they are trying to tell you.

Non-identification – realize that these thoughts and feelings are not you, that they may be present in this moment, but are just passing through.

At the risk of repeating myself, I'll stress again that it's best to start with the small stuff, as you re-create difficult situations, moments of conflict or distressing encounters. Don't dive straight in, and take yourself immediately back to a key moment of trauma from your childhood – or from any other time in your life; don't try to get to the heart of all your difficulties and problems in one fell swoop. As with the practice of mindfulness itself, recognize that these things take time, and that this is a gentle, ongoing process: a gradual, controlled and compassionate exploration of your inner landscape.

> *'Ultimately, happiness comes down to choosing between the discomfort of becoming aware of your mental afflictions and the discomfort of being ruled by them.'*
> Yongey Mingyur Rinpoche[10]

You now have all the tools to begin your journey to a life lived mindfully and with awareness, one where you are not pushed and pulled around by your thoughts and feelings. Here you will find great peace, and along the way you will discover that you have the ability to end much of your own suffering, and that you will in turn cause much less suffering to those you love and care about. You will gain insights and realizations about yourself and the world around you that will astound you.

Ultimately, you will see how to stop limiting yourself by not identifying who you are with how you feel or think. Once you truly know this, you will find that you can never be *just* happy or sad or lonely or anxious or anything else, no matter how hard you try – because you are the incredible, vast awareness *in which* all these experiences, and everything else, exist.

You will quickly come to see that the thoughts and sensations, feelings and emotions you have are merely visitors which stay with you only fleetingly, until the next experience takes their place. All of this happens through the simple practice of mindfulness – 20 minutes of mindful meditation in the morning and evening, every day, and the continuing effort to bring more and more mindful moments and ways of being into your day-to-day life.

One of the most important gifts greater awareness brings is the realization that your mind is not a thing located somewhere in your body. (If it was, doctors would have found it by now!)

Your mind is an ever expanding,
all-encompassing awareness
through which you experience
yourself and the world around you,
and the only person who can limit
your mind, and its awareness, is you.

Throughout this book, we have explored the powerful way in which the practice of mindfulness works to naturally build your compassion for others, and for yourself. With increased awareness comes the knowledge that we all share the same wish – to be free from suffering. This beautiful meditation allows us to give voice to that wish, and to strengthen our resolve to do what we can to achieve this freedom for ourselves and others.

Loving-Kindness Meditation

Sit quietly on your cushion or chair, relax your body and allow your eyes to close gently. Bring your focus and awareness to your breath, and wherever in the body you feel it most.

Call to mind someone you love and care for deeply and allow a picture of them to form. Remember why you feel so much love for this person. As you generate a feeling of great love and kindness towards them in this way, send them the following blessing:

> *May you be happy*
> *May you be healthy*
> *May you be safe*
> *May you live with ease*

Now, allow yourself to recognize that you yourself are worthy and deserving of exactly the same in your life. Focusing all your love and kindness on yourself, make the same wish for your own life:

> *May I be happy*
> *May I be healthy*
> *May I be safe*
> *May I live in peace*

Finally, picture all living beings everywhere, and offer the same blessing to them:

May they be happy
May they be healthy
May they be safe
May they live with ease

Epilogue

The Boy from Kota Kinabalu

*'Great things are done by a series of
small things brought together.'*

<small>Vincent van Gogh</small>

About 15 years ago, my wife Faye (then my girlfriend) and I went to Borneo. We didn't have kids at the time so were able to take the adventurous option of trekking through the jungles of this beautiful island. This was an experience that I won't forget quickly. We don't have a lot of jungle in Ireland, and being immersed in one feels totally alien and at the same time amazing. Butterflies the size of small plates flutter by, painted in the most vibrant and striking colours. Everywhere there are insects which look like they have been exposed to some type of size-enhancing radiation. By day, it is hot and humid and at night, you hear sounds that would keep the bravest soul wide awake and on guard. But the heat and tiredness disappear when you come face to face with the 'orange man of Borneo' – the beautiful orangutan. I still don't know who was more surprised – Faye and I, or the orangutans. I definitely know that we were the more awestruck.

When our jungle adventure had finished, we decided to spend a week relaxing in the Tanjung Aru area, just outside the city of Kota Kinabalu, which is known locally and by tourists to the area as 'KK'. One evening, after spending the day in the city, we wandered down to the waterfront, planning to walk along the boardwalk as dusk fell. This area is full of lively bars and restaurants and market stalls selling street food, with a wonderful, eclectic mix of cultures as well as an old-world-meets-new vibe.

After a short stroll, we found a table outside one of the bars, and sat for a while in the middle of all this bustle, taking in the sights and watching the human drama unfold. As we sat there, Faye caught a whiff of freshly made doughnuts. We were both feeling quite hungry by this stage – and so she declared she was going to locate the source of the delicious smell, promising to bring something back for me too. Meanwhile, I ordered a beer and sat happily, just soaking in the atmosphere of the place.

All at once I noticed a young boy – he must have been around 11 or 12 years old – emerging from the crowd and heading very decisively in my direction. Local kids approaching foreigners to sell stuff was common enough, so I thought I knew what his purpose was. I watched him as he made his way towards me, and I noticed he wasn't carrying anything to sell. His eyes firmly fixed on me, he approached my table. With a serious yet friendly expression on his face, he began to speak. Something in his manner and the tone of his voice gave me the distinct impression that whatever he was saying was very important and that I should be paying close attention. The problem however was that I didn't speak Malay and that, clearly, he didn't speak English. After about two or three minutes of him talking, looking at me intently as he did so, he fell silent. He then nodded, smiled, and set his hand on my head, before disappearing back into the bustle of the market in the same direction as he had come from.

After this strange encounter, I simply sat there for a time, gazing after the boy and wondering about what had just happened. *Who was he? What was that all about?* And most importantly of all – *what on earth had he just said to me?* He'd seemed so earnest and well-meaning, and what he'd told me was clearly very important to him. When Faye came back with a couple of hot, fragrant doughnuts wrapped in buttery paper, I told her what had just happened. We both puzzled for a while over what the young boy might possibly have said, and then forgot all about it, as we decided to head back to where we were staying in Tanjung Aru and sort out something for dinner.

However, in the days, months, and indeed years that followed, my mind would return to that boy every so often, and the intent expression in his eyes and the apparent importance of what he felt he just had to tell me. I decided that there were only two possible explanations. The first was that I had been given some extremely profound message about life – of which, sadly, I had not been able to understand a single word. The second possibility was that I had had a wasp – or perhaps some even more exotic and dangerous insect – perched on my head, and that the boy felt he needed to point this out to me and warn me of the danger.

I am fully aware of course that there could have been a million other explanations for this strange encounter – but for whatever reason, these are the two I chose. With the passing of time, I have found that, of the two, I prefer to believe the 'profound message' explanation. I also like to think that whatever that important and highly significant message was, and in spite of the language chasm, I was somehow able to take it on board. I'm not of course expecting you to go along with this perhaps fanciful and even slightly odd way of thinking, but just, I suppose, to accept that this is what I have chosen to believe.

All these years later, I can think of nothing that has changed my life so profoundly for the better than the practice of mindfulness and the effort to increase my awareness. And so, thinking back now to that young boy in Kota Kinabalu, I like to believe that the message he had for me was this: 'You are missing your life, and your head is full of suffering. Start your practice and you will suffer less and be less of an assh**e!' And clearly, at some level, it seems I was able to understand this message, because, just a few years later, that's exactly what I did to try to change my way of living.

And so, just like the message from the boy in Kota Kinabalu, even if it didn't always make sense at the time, I greatly hope that this book has had something positive to offer you. I sincerely wish that, even if you haven't found anything profound in these pages, you may at least have found something useful. I am very much aware that others may be able to deliver this message better, but my hope is that my main purpose, which was to above all be useful and to share with you what has worked, and still works, for me, has in some way been realized. For anyone who commits to them, the practice of mindfulness and the development of awareness has profound benefits – not least of which is so much less personal suffering for us and for those that we love.

As I have said many times throughout this book, the work is not in the least difficult – 20 minutes of formal meditation twice a day, and the simple effort of bringing awareness to what you already do in your daily life. It's simple, but please don't dismiss it because of this. Its benefits are not simple or superficial – they are nothing less than life-changing.

I have tried my best to convey how profoundly my practice has helped me, and now I wish and pray that you may enjoy the same journey. I want you to experience the sheer joy of impermanence. I want you to be free from the grip of fear, worry, guilt, anxiety and the myriad of other sufferings that can blight our wonderful human existence. I want you to see the joy in the everyday things we normally miss. I want you to truly be acquainted with the earth-shattering realization that you are not separate or isolated, but intimately connected to everybody and everything in this life.

The truth, though, is that my wanting this for you will not deliver it to you. If you want things to be different, you have to change something. So, please, go ahead and start your practice now. Don't wait for a better time, because a better time than right now doesn't exist.

This works. I am living proof of the fact – and if I can do it, I know that you can!

May you be happy

May you be healthy

May you be safe

May you live with ease

Namaste.

Paddy Brosnan

Any merit obtained from this work is dedicated to all sentient beings. Due to this merit, may all beings be released from their suffering and abide in happiness forever.

References

1. Atman translates as eternal consciousness.

2. www.psychologytoday.com/us/blog/the-mindful-self-express/201704/stuck-in-negative-thinking-it-could-be-your-brain (accessed 1 May 2018).

3. Yangmei, L. Kong, F. et al. 'Resting state functional connectivity of the default mode network associated with happiness', *Social Cognitive and Affective Neuroscience*, 2016; 11(3): 516–24.

4. Farewell Letter to the Tergar Community from Mingyur Rinpoche: https://tergar.org/communities-and-practice-groups/letter-from-yongey-mingyur-rinpoche-before-entering-retreat (accessed 1 May 2018).

5. 2016 Report: Mindful Nation UK – local councils finding value in mindfulness as a way of tackling those who are long term unemployed, and problems such as drug addiction.

6. https://bebrainfit.com/the-health-benefits-of-art-are-for-everyone (accessed 1 May 2018).

7. www.telegraph.co.uk/science/2017/08/06/loneliness-deadlier-obesity-study-suggests (accessed 1 May 2018).

8. http://tinyurl.com/ycc4on62 (accessed 1 May 2018).

9. www.cancer.net/survivorship/life-after-cancer/post-traumatic-stress-disorder-and-cancer (accessed 1 May 2018).

10. Rinpoche, Y. M. and Swanson, E., 2010. *The Joy of Living*. Transworld Digital.

ABOUT THE AUTHOR

Patrick Murphy

Paddy Brosnan is a mindfulness and meditation teacher, inspirational speaker and author.

In his early 30s Paddy experienced a radical shift in how he wanted to live his life. This marked the beginning of an intense inward journey of spiritual development. He left the business world and devoted the following years to developing his awareness through the practice of mindfulness and meditation, and is honoured to include The Venerable Thich Nhat Hanh and The Venerable Panchen Ötrul Rinpoche among his teachers and inspirations. In the years since, he has devoted himself to understanding and deepening this transformation.

Paddy's teachings are simple but at the same time profound. At the heart of this is a very direct and accessible insight into how the development of awareness can ultimately bring us a deeper sense of contentment and happiness. This simple message, delivered with humour and compassion, has helped countless people find inner peace and fulfilment in their lives.

Paddy is a sought-after public speaker and travels extensively to deliver workshops and retreats, as well as visiting schools to encourage mindfulness in children.

www.paddybrosnan.com

Hay House Podcasts
Bring Fresh, Free Inspiration Each Week!

Hay House proudly offers a selection of life-changing audio content via our most popular podcasts!

Hay House Meditations Podcast

Features your favorite Hay House authors guiding you through meditations designed to help you relax and rejuvenate. Take their words into your soul and cruise through the week!

Dr. Wayne W. Dyer Podcast

Discover the timeless wisdom of Dr. Wayne W. Dyer, world-renowned spiritual teacher and affectionately known as "the father of motivation." Each week brings some of the best selections from the 10-year span of Dr. Dyer's talk show on HayHouseRadio.com.

Hay House World Summit Podcast

Over 1 million people from 217 countries and territories participate in the massive online event known as the Hay House World Summit. This podcast offers weekly mini-lessons from World Summits past as a taste of what you can hear during the annual event, which occurs each May.

Hay House Radio Podcast

Listen to some of the best moments from HayHouseRadio.com, featuring expert authors such as Dr. Christiane Northrup, Anthony William, Caroline Myss, James Van Praagh, and Doreen Virtue discussing topics such as health, self-healing, motivation, spirituality, positive psychology, and personal development.

Hay House Live Podcast

Enjoy a selection of insightful and inspiring lectures from Hay House Live, an exciting event series that features Hay House authors and leading experts in the fields of alternative health, nutrition, intuitive medicine, success, and more! Feel the electricity of our authors engaging with a live audience, and get motivated to live your best life possible!

Find Hay House podcasts on iTunes, or visit www.HayHouse.com/podcasts for more info.

HAY HOUSE

Look within

Join the conversation about latest products,
events, exclusive offers and more.

 Hay House UK

 @HayHouseUK

 @hayhouseuk

♥ healyourlife.com

We'd love to hear from you!